POEMS

BY

MISS H. F. GOULD.

POEMS

BY

MISS H. F. GOULD.

VOLUME II.

BOSTON:
HILLIARD, GRAY & CO.

1836.

FREEMAN AND BOLLES,
Printers....Washington street.

TO

MRS. HANNAH F. LEE,

AS A TOKEN OF

Sincere Attachment,

THIS LITTLE VOLUME

IS AFFECTIONATELY

INSCRIBED.

CONTENTS.

POEMS.

THE LAKE OF KILLARNEY.

In Erin's verdant, ocean isle,
  A shining lake is seen,
Where many an islet peers the while,
  To stud the lake with green.

And these are crowned with tree and flower,
  And vine, or ruins gray,
That show where human art and power
  Have been, and past away.

They 're edged with grass, or fringing brake,
  Or moss, or beetling cliff;
And, round between them, on the lake
  There dances many a skiff.

The boatman's hardy hand propels
  His boat with varying oar,
While stories wild and strange he tells,
  About the things of yore.

And, if you touch that hand with gold
  Or silver, you shall find,
A smoother tale was never told,
  Than he will soon unwind.

But then no sign of secret doubt,
  About what may be said,
From lip or eye must venture out,
  As this would snap the thread.

For, though he may in truth believe
  The things he tells to you,
Or not, 't is fit that you receive
  Each syllable as true.

In sooth, the honest boatman seems
  A man sincere, and acts
Like one, who, often telling dreams,
  Refines them into facts.

He 'll take you in his boat and row
  Till fairly from the shore;
Then fast his nimble tongue will go,
  And slow the lazy oar.

And there, in haste to let you know
  How much is known to him,
He 'll tell you what is hid below
  The water that you skim.

For, how Killarney's lake arose,
  His sober lips protest,

That, if a son of Erin knows,
  Himself must know the best.

And having paid his holy priest
  For past and future sins,
And lived a saint through lent and feast,
  The tale he thus begins:

'You see that in this spacious cave
  There 's now a mighty flood;
But once, as you 've a soul to save,
  'T was full of flesh and blood!

'And now I row my trusty boat
  O'er heaps of human bones,
That, by the waters where we float,
  Are hardened into stones!

'For, here an ancient city shone
  In splendor, wealth, and pride;
And that in power it stood alone,
  Can be by none denied.

''T was peopled by a noble clan
  Of brave and warlike men;
If ever Erin had a man
  Of courage, it was then.

''T was governed by a mighty chief,
  The great O'Donaghue;
And just to give him in the brief,
  A mighty tyrant, too!

'He was a man of giant size,
  Of odd, but rich attire,
With haughty bearing, and his eyes,—
  They flashed like living fire.

'He often led his men to fight,
  And led them safely back;
But left the foes, that lived in flight,
  With blood upon their track.

'For when they saw his hordes advance,
  And knew him in the van,
His very look was like a lance,
  To enter every man.

'His eye was worth a thousand shafts,
  A thousand arms, his one!
His will was like the wing that wafts
  The eagle to the sun!

'And such the great O'Donaghue;
  And such the race of men,
Whose like, if e'er creation knew,
  'T will never know again!

'And all that mortals ever need
  This noble clan possessed;
For they had all to clothe and feed,
  And give the body rest.

'But, still they lacked one thing, and this,
  The burden of their song,

Was what no living thing can miss,
  And live to miss it long.

'And "water! water!" they would sing,
  And some for water call.
They 'd neither well, nor brook, nor spring,
  Within their city wall.

'At length, without, the streams were dry
  That brightened vale and hill,
And then, from thirsty mouths, the cry
  Was "water! water!" still.

'There came a great magician there,
  A man of power and skill,
Who had the gift to answer prayer,
  And do the suppliant's will.

'To him in crowds the people came,
  As pilgrims to a shrine:
Approaching in St. Patrick's name,
  The man of gifts divine.

'And water, water, was the thing
  For which they humbly bowed,
Entreating him the boon to bring
  From either earth or cloud.

'But still he answered not their call;
  For in his searching sight,
There was not one among them all
  Who asked that boon aright.

'At length a little soft-eyed maid,
 With looks and voice to melt
A rock to water, came and prayed,
 And asking water, knelt.

'A ring the great magician wore,
 Of gems so clear and bright,
They looked like drops of dew before
 The rays of morning light.

'Then, in the earth, from off his hand,
 He hid the sparkling ring,
When, straightway from the burning sand
 Came forth a cooling spring!

'And every one with parching lip,
 Who ran to fill his cup,
Perceived that, fast as all could dip,
 The water bubbled up.

'The great magician said, the spring
 Must every night, with care,
Be covered close, or it would bring
 An evil none could bear.

'And thus to let the spring be hid,
 He gave a shining gift—
A large and massive silver lid,
 That none alone could lift.

'Upon its surface smooth and bright,
 Were strange devices traced;

And o'er the water every night,
   With care 't was closely placed.

'At morning it wss set aside
   To let the spring appear,
And all the city was supplied
   With water fresh and clear.

'At length, the proud O'Donaghue
   Began to jeer and scoff,
Because the cover must go through
   This putting on and off.

' "I 'll to my dwelling bid them take
   The shining lid," said he,
"And turn it upside down, to make
   A silver bath for me."

'He ordered then his men to bring
   The cover home to him;
And quick with water from the spring
   To fill it to the brim.

'But all implored him not to touch
   The lid with this intent,
Because the giver's charge was such
   They dreaded what it meant.

' "Away!" replied the chief, in wrath,
   "Ye cowards, from my sight!
For I will have my silver bath
   Before I sleep to-night.

' "So off, to get the cover, go!
The water will but be
The cooler, if the night winds blow
Upon it fresh and free."

'Then, when they went, as they were bid,
To do the stern commands,
It set the figures on the lid
To stirring in their hands.

'And reptile, bird, and beast began
To move, and writhe, and twist,
As if to caution every man
Who bore them, to desist!

'The scaly serpent showed a sting,
And, hissing, seemed to say,
They 'd rue the hour, when from the spring
They bore the lid away.

'When, by their chief, with water filled,
They left it, to retire,
Their breasts were some with horror chilled,
And others burnt with ire.

'But every clansman sought his home,
And saw the fall of night,
With gloomy thoughts of what might come
Before the morning light.

'They feared that earthquake, fire, or wind,
Or famine, or the sword,

Would punish all who did not mind
  The great magician's word.

'Then one sad, solitary man
  Escaped from out the gate,
And, to a hill, in secret, ran,
  To mark the city's fate.

'At midnight hour, when all was still,
  And not a leaf was stirred,
That lonely watchman on the hill,
  The shrieks of anguish heard.

'And "water! water!" was the cry,
  That from the city broke,
In voices that were wild and high,
  And mortal terror spoke.

'It was a solemn, awful sound,
  For one alone to hear,
As through the hills it echoed round,
  Then died upon the ear.

''T was but a little while, and all
  Was over with the clan!
For not within the city wall
  Was there a living man!

'The spring had bubbled up and swelled,
  And to a deluge spread,
Till now the silent dwellings held
  But water and the dead!

'And still the waters spread and grew,
  Till in a single night,
This mighty lake arose to view,
  A city sunk from sight!

'And, when the deep is calm and clear,
  These little isles between
The walls and dwellings buried here,
  May yet, in part, be seen.

'But often, when the raging storm
  Is now about to wake,
A cloudy boat and spirit form
  Will sail above the lake.

'They say, 't is old O'Donaghue,
  Who haunts the waters still,
And having nothing good to do,
  Is busied yet with ill.

'The costly bath, wherein he died,
  Is turned to silver mist;
But still upon its bright outside
  The serpents crawl and twist.

'The boatmen shun his troubled path
  Across the frowning flood,
For he is still a son of wrath,
  Though not of flesh and blood!

'On yonder rock there sits a man,
  Who saw him yesterday,

An hour before the storm began,
   That drove his boat away!

'Now, when your honor likes to take
   Another pleasant sail,
To view the islands of the lake,
   I 'll tell another tale.'

THE STARS AND THE FALLING DEW.

The sun, like a hero, whose chariot rolled
In glory, has reached the west;
And wrapped in his mantle of crimson and gold,
Has sunken away to rest.
The stars from the skies
Look forth like the eyes
Of Angels, the earth to view;
While timid and soft,
Their light form aloft,
Comes down with the falling dew.

The flowers, that, oppressed by the monarch of day,
Have bowing confessed his power,
Are lifting their foreheads, relieved of his ray,
To the cool of the evening hour.
And each holding up
Her emerald cup,
Her delicate draught to renew,
Their trust is repaid,
While their thirst is allayed
By the drops of the falling dew.

The birds are at rest in their own little homes,
Their songs are forgotten in sleep;
And low and uncertain the murmuring comes
From over the slumbering deep.

The breezes that sighed
Have fainted and died
In the boughs they were quivering through,
And motion and sound
Have ceased from around
To yield to the falling dew.

And gently it comes, as the shadowy wing
Of night o'er the earth is unfurled;
A silent, refreshing and spirit-like thing,
To brighten and solace the world!
As the face of a friend,
When in sorrow we bend—
Like a heart ever tender and true,
When darkness is ours,
To the earth and the flowers,
Are the stars and the falling dew.

THE GRASSHOPPER AND THE ANT.

'Ant, look at me!' a young Grasshopper said,
As nimbly he sprang from his green, summer bed,
'See how I 'm going to skip over your head,
    And could o'er a thousand like you!
Ant, by your motion alone, I should judge
That Nature ordained you a slave and a drudge,
For ever and ever to keep on the trudge,
    And always find something to do.

'Oh! there is nothing like having our day,
Taking our pleasure and ease while we may,
Bathing ourselves in the bright, mellow ray
    That comes from the warm, golden sun!
While I am up in the light and the air,
You, a sad picture of labor and care!
Still have some hard, heavy burden to bear,
    And work that you never get done.

'I have an exercise healthful, and good,
For tuning the nerves and digesting the food —
Graceful gymnastics for stirring the blood
    Without the gross purpose of use.
Ant, let me tell you 't is not *à la mode*,
To plod like a pilgrim and carry a load,
Perverting the limbs that for grace were bestowed,
    By such a plebeian abuse.

'While the whole world with provisions is filled,
Who would keep toiling and toiling to build
And lay in a store for himself, till he 's killed
With work that another might do?
Come! drop your budget and just give a spring.
Jump on a grass-blade and balance and swing.
Soon you 'll be light as a gnat on the wing,
Gay as a grasshopper, too!'

Ant trudged along while the grasshopper sung,
Minding her business and holding her tongue,
Until she got home her own people among;
But these were her thoughts on the road.
'What will become of that poor, idle one
When the light sports of the summer are done?
And, where is the covert to which he may run
To find a safe winter abode?

'Oh! if I only could tell him how sweet
Toil makes my rest and the morsel I eat,
While hope gives a spur to my little black feet,
He 'd never pity my lot!
He 'd never ask me my burden to drop
To join in his folly — to spring, and to hop;
And thus make the ant and her labor to stop,
When time, I am certain, would not.

'When the cold frost all the herbage has nipped,
When the bare branches with ice-drops are tipped,
Where will the grasshopper then be, that skipped,
So careless and lightly to-day?

Frozen to-death! '*a sad picture*' indeed,
Of reckless indulgence and what must succeed,
That all his gymnastics ca 'nt shelter or feed,
Or quicken his pulse into play.

'I must prepare for a winter to come.
I shall be glad of a home and a crumb,
When my frail form out of doors would be numb,
And I in the snow-storm should die.
Summer is lovely, but soon will be past.
Summer has plenty not always to last.
Summer 's the time for the ant to make fast
Her stores for a future supply!'

THE CATERPILLAR.

'Don't kill me!' Caterpillar said,
  As Charles had raised his heel
Upon the humble worm to tread,
  As though it could not feel.

'Don't kill me! and I'll crawl away
  To hide awhile, and try
To come and look, another day,
  More pleasing to your eye.

'I know I'm now among the things
  Uncomely to your sight;
But by and by on splendid wings
  You'll see me high and light!

'And then, perhaps, you may be glad
  To watch me on the flower;
And that you spared the worm you had
  To-day within your power!'

Then Caterpillar went and hid
  In some secreted place,
Where none could look on what he did
  To change his form and face.

And by and by, when Charles had quite
  Forgotten what I 've told,
A Butterfly appeared in sight
  Most beauteous to behold.

His shining wings were trimmed with gold,
  And many a brilliant dye
Was laid upon their velvet fold,
  To charm the gazing eye!

Then, near as prudence would allow,
  To Charles's ear he drew
And said, 'You may not know me, now
  My form and name are new!

'But I'm the worm that once you raised
  Your ready foot to kill!
For sparing me, I long have praised,
  And love and praise you still.

'The lowest reptile at your feet,
  When power is not abused,
May prove the fruit of mercy sweet,
  By being kindly used!'

THE CAPTIVE BUTTERFLY.

Good morning, pretty Butterfly!
  How have you passed the night?
I hope you 're gay and glad as I
  To see the morning light.

But, little silent one, methinks
  You 're in a sober mood.
I wonder if you 'd like to drink,
  And what you take for food.

I shut you in my crystal cup
  To let your winglets rest.
And now I want to hold you up,
  To see your velvet vest.

I want to count your tiny toes,
  To find your breathing-place,
And touch the downy horn that grows
  Each side your pretty face.

I 'd like to see just how you 're made,
  With streaks and spots and rings;
And wish you 'd show me how you played
  Your shining, rainbow wings.

'’T was not,' the little prisoner said,
'For want of food or drink,
That, while you slumbered on your bed,
I could not sleep a wink.

'My wings are pained for want of flight,
My lungs, for want of air.
In bitterness I've passed the night,
And meet the morning's glare.

'When looking through my prison wall,
So close and yet so clear,
I see there's freedom there for all,
While I'm a captive here.

'I've stood upon my feeble feet
Until they're full of pain.
I know that liberty is sweet,
Which I cannot regain.

'Do I deserve a fate like this,
Who've ever acted well,
Since first I left the chrysalis,
And fluttered from my shell?

'I've never injured fruit, or flower,
Or man, or bird, or beast;
And such a one should have the power
Of going free, at least.

'And now, if you will let me quit
  My prison-house, the cup,
I 'll show you how I sport and flit,
  And make my wings go up!'

The lid was raised; the prisoner said,
  'Behold my airy play!'
Then quickly on the wing he fled
  Away, away, away!

From flower to flower he gaily flew,
  To cool his aching feet
And slake his thirst with morning dew,
  Where liberty was sweet,

THE BEE, CLOVER, AND THISTLE.

A **Bee** from her hive one morning flew,
    A tune to the day-light humming;
And away she went, o'er the clear, bright dew,
Where the grass was green, the violet blue,
    And the gold of the sun was coming.

And what first tempted the roving Bee
    Was a head of the crimson clover.
'I've found a treasure betimes!' said she,
'And perhaps a greater I might not see,
    If I travelled the field all over.

'My beautiful clover, so round and red,
    There is not a thing in twenty
That lifts this morning so sweet a head
Above its leaves and its earthy bed,
    With so many horns of plenty!'

The flow'rets were thick, which the clover crowned,
    As the plumes in the helm of Hector,
And each had a cell that was deep and round;
Yet it would not impart, as the bee soon found,
    One drop of its precious nectar.

She cast in her eye where the honey lay,
    And her pipe she began to measure;
But she saw at once it was clear as day,
That it would not go down one half the way
    To the place of the envied treasure.

Said she in a pet, 'one thing I know,'
As she rose in haste and departed,
'It is not those of the greatest *show*,
To whom for a favor 't is best to go,
Or that prove most generous-hearted!'

A fleecy flock came into the field,
And one of its members followed
The scent of the clover, till between
Her nibbling teeth its head was seen,
And then in a moment swallowed.

'Ha, ha!' said the Bee, as the clover died,
'Her fortune's smile was fickle!
And now I can get my wants supplied
By a humble flower with a rough outside,
And even a scale and prickle.'

Then she flew to one that by man and beast
Was shunned for its pointed bristle;
But it injured not the bee in the least;
And she filled her pocket, and had a feast
From the bloom of the purple Thistle.

The generous Thistle's life was spared
In the home where the Bee first found her;
Till she grew so old she was hoary-haired,
And her snow-white locks with the silk compared,
As they shone where the sun beamed round her.

THE WILD VIOLET.

VIOLET, violet, sparkling with dew,
Down in the meadow-land wild where you grew,
How did you come by the beautiful blue
With which your soft petals unfold?
And how do you hold up your tender, young head
When rude, sweeping winds rush along o'er your bed,
And dark, gloomy clouds ranging over you shed
Their waters so heavy and cold?

No one has nursed you, or watched you an hour,
Or found you a place in the garden or bower;
And they cannot yield me so lovely a flower,
As here I have found at my feet!
Speak, my sweet violet! answer and tell
How you have grown up and flourished so well,
And look so contented where lowly you dwell,
And we thus by accident meet!

'The same careful hand,' the Violet said,
'That holds up the firmament, holds up my head!
And He, who with azure the skies overspread,
Has painted the violet blue.
He sprinkles the stars out above me by night,
And sends down the sunbeams at morning with light
To make my new coronet sparkling and bright,
When formed of a drop of his dew!

'I 've nought to fear from the black, heavy cloud,
Or the breath of the tempest that comes strong and
loud!
Where, born in the lowland, and far from the crowd,
I know, and I live but for ONE.
He soon forms a mantle about me to cast,
Of long, silken grass, till the rain and the blast,
And all that seemed threatening have harmlessly
passed,
As the clouds scud before the warm sun!'

THE DYING LAMP.

Poor Dying Lamp! thou now art low and pale;
 Thine oil of life is out, thy purpose o'er;
And thou art fainting, utterly to fail;
 In a few moments thou must be no more!

The morning star has risen, and the dawn
 Hastens to chase the scattering shades away.
They and thy feeble flame will soon be gone,
 And both forgotten in the glorious day.

Well—thou hast done a kindly work to-night,
 And freely worn thyself away to shed
Through the dark, silent chamber thy soft light,
 And show the watcher to the sick one's bed.

A mild, bright minister of good to man,
 Wasting thyself for others, thou hast been,
Since with the evening thy short life began,
 Till o'er the world the light of heaven pours in.

But now thou art not needed thus to cast
 Thy beams around to cheer the wakeful eye;
Since darkness with its solemn reign is past,
 Before the morning calmly dost thou die.

Like thee, may she, who marked thy steady ray
   Through the hushed night, and then thy quick de-
      cline,
Yield, while she treads life's short and shadowy way,
   Some cheering light, with purpose pure as thine!

Then, when her work is finished — when her worth
   To others in their dark, sad hours shall cease,
Not to survive it, may she pass from earth,
   And like her dying lamp go out in peace!

THE BRIDEMAID.

'T is over! I have past the cruel test!
Methinks I carried well the mask of joy,
That frequent use had fitted to my face
Too closely to be shaken by the throb
Of a torn bosom. Yes, I chose the dove
To fasten at my breast this chain of gems,
A sign of peace within. Sad mockery!
The *dove* was all without, and formed of stone!
A heart that 's breaking at another's bliss
Should burst without a groan; and mine I thank,
That every string has snapped so silently,
Quivered and bled unseen.
                              Ye beauteous flowers,
Behold your sisters in the cast-off wreath,
That, pale and worthless, withers at my feet!
They speak of her who wore them — Ye, of one
Who grew beside her: Yet, the dew of grief
Ne'er touched her bloom.
                              My silent lute, farewell!
Thy broken strings will never be restored.
When next thy mistress sweeps the tuneful chord,
May seraph voices mingle with the notes
Where sorrow claims no strain!
                              Poor, sickly pearls!
How dim and pale ye look, trailed useless out!
The hue of death is cast o'er every thing;
And, *vanity* is marked on all I see.

On all! Oh, no! One blessed sign appears,
A precious emblem to the eye of Faith!
The holy cross, formed of these ocean gems.
Lo! what a sudden lustre they assume!
It came not from the deep! It is the smile
Of heaven upon the figure they show forth!
With this before me, shall not purer love
And higher hopes than feed on aught below
Lead home my wildered soul?
If Heaven will take
A heart that earth has crushed, form it anew,
And light it from on high, I offer mine,
Not without shame, that all things else were tried
Before the only balm.
Look down, O Thou,
Who wast at Cana! Bless the rite that 's past!
Help me to put a wedding garment on
For the great marriage supper; and to wear
Thy choice of ornaments, while I await
The coming of the BRIDEGROOM!

THE MEETING.

We met upon Mount Auburn, ere its sod
Was strewed with drops from sorrow's languid eye;
Before its shadowy walks the mourner trod,
Or to its balmy air released the sigh.

The spot had just been rendered hallowed ground,
By solemn rite and consecrating prayer;
It bore no marble, heaved no sacred mound,
But Nature reigned in placid beauty there.

And as we stood, and viewed the peaceful scene,
Our thought and converse on its purpose ran;
And on the swiftness of the race, between
The point of starting, and the goal of man.

He plucked for me a branch, where wide and high
The thick, green boughs around us hung a shade,
But thought not, that his lips and beaming eye
Must close for ever, ere its leaves should fade.

We never met again! The branch retained
Its verdure, when his eye had lost its light.
The vital flame within his bosom waned,
And left it cold, while yet my branch was bright.

A few short days — and he was on the deep,
Whose swelling surges he should cross no more.
In foreign earth the stranger's ashes sleep —
His spirit walks the everlasting shore!

But, we shall meet again! While, 'dust to dust,'
Of this frail house of clay may soon be said,
Its tenant His unfailing word will trust,
Whose second coming shall revive the dead.

On that great morning may our meeting be
Among the flowery hills without a grave,
And in the shade of that unfading Tree,
Whose boughs with healing for the nations wave!

THE YOUNG SETTING MOON.

The fair, young moon in a silver bow,
  Looks back from the bending west,
Like a weary soul, that is glad to go
  To the long-sought place of rest.

Her crescent lies in a beaming crown
  On the distant hill's dark head,
Serene as the righteous looking down
  On the world, from his dying bed.

Her rays, to our view, grow few and faint.
  Her light is at last withdrawn;
And she, like the calmly departing saint,
  To her far-off home is gone.

O! what could have made the moon so bright
  Till her work for the earth was done?
'T was the glory drawn from a purer light —
  From the face of the radiant sun!

For she on her absent king could look,
  Whom the world saw not the while;
Her face from his all its beauty took —
  She conveyed to the world his smile.

By him, through night has the moon been led
  'Mid the clouds that crossed the sky,
While she drew her beams o'er the earth to shed,
  From the god where she fixed her eye.

And thus does Faith 'mid her trials, view
  In the God to whom she clings
A Sun, whose glories for ever new,
  Unfold in his healing wings.

'T is He, who will guide our course aright
  Though grief overcloud the heart;
And it is but faith being lost in sight
  When the good from the earth depart!

THE HIDDEN NAME.

She loved; but her bosom had buried the dart;
  And there, while she strove to conceal it,
Its point had engraven his NAME on her heart
  Too deep for her lips to reveal it.

She wept; but the world knew it not, for her eye,
  Of joy's playful sunlight would borrow
A few dazzling beams, when another was by,
  To drink up the dew-drops of sorrow.

She grieved; and in secret the sigh would release,
  That long in her breast had been stifled.
She pined; and in solitude mourned for the peace,
Whereof her young heart had been rifled.

She languished and faded, and silently fell;
  And now in the tomb she is lying.
While none that looked on could the malady tell,
  The flower in its beauty was dying!

But told was her secret on many a leaf,
  While cold was the hand that conveyed it.
In lines that were broken and blotted with grief,
  Where Death, a pale spoiler! betrayed it.

And yet, not a trace of the NAME can be found;
  With darkness and silence hung o'er it,
The sacred engraving is hid in the ground,
  Locked up in the bosom that bore it!

THE OLD ELM OF NEWBURY.

Did ever it come in your way to pass
The silvery pond with its fringe of grass;
And, threading the lane hard by, to see
The veteran Elm of Newbury?

You saw how its roots had grasped the ground
As if it had felt that the earth went round,
And fastened them down with determined will
To keep it steady, and hold it still.
Its aged trunk, so stately and strong
Has braved the blasts as they 've rushed along,
Its head has towered, and its arms have spread,
While more than a hundred years have fled!

Well, that old elm, that is now so grand,
Was once a twig in the rustic hand
Of a youthful peasant, who went one night
To visit his love, by the tender light
Of the modest moon and her twinkling host,
While the star that lighted his bosom most,
And gave to his lonely feet their speed,
Abode in a cottage beyond the mead!

'T was the peaceful close of a summer's day;
Its glorious orb had passed away;
The toil of the field till the morn had ceased,
For a season of rest to man and beast.

The mother had silenced her humming wheel;
The father returned for the evening meal,
The thanks of one who had chosen the part
Of the poor in spirit, the rich in heart,
Who, having the soul's grand panacea,
Feel all is added that 's needful here;
And know this truth of the human breast,
That, *wanting little, is being blest.*
The good old man in his chair reclined,
At a humble door, with a peaceful mind,
While the drops from his sun-burnt brow were dried
By the cool, sweet air of the eventide.

The son from the yoke had unlocked the bow,
Dismissing the faithful ox to go
And graze in the close. He had called the kine
For their oblation at day's decline.
He 'd gathered and numbered the lambs and sheep,
And fastened them up in their nightly keep.
He 'd stood by the coop till the hen could bring
Her huddling brood safe under her wing;
And made them secure from the hooting owl,
Whose midnight prey was the shrieking fowl.
When all was finished, he sped to the well
Where the old gray bucket hastily fell,
And the clear cold water came up to chase
The dust of the field from his neck and face,
And hands and feet, till the youth began
To look renewed in the outer man;
And soon arrayed in his Sunday's best,
The stiff new suit had done the rest;

And the hale, young lover was on his way,
Where, through the fen and the field it lay;
And over the bramble, the brake and the grass,
As the shortest cut to the house of his lass.

It is not recorded how long he staid
In the cheerful home of the smiling maid;
But when he came out, it was late and dark,
And silent — not even a dog would bark,
To take from his feeling of loneliness,
And make the length of his way seem less.
He thought it was strange, that the treacherous moon
Should have given the world the slip so soon;
And, whether the eyes of the girl had made
The stars of the sky in his own to fade,
Or not, it certainly seemed to him,
That each grew distant, and small, and dim;
And he shuddered to think he now was about
To take a long and a lonely route;
For he did not know what fearful sight
Might come to him through the shadows of night!

An Elm grew close by the cottage's eaves;
So, he plucked him a twig well clothed with leaves,
And sallying forth with the supple arm,
To serve as a talisman parrying harm,
He felt that, though his heart was so big,
'T was even the stouter for having the twig.
For this, he thought, would answer to switch
The horrors away, as he crossed the ditch,

The meadow and copse, wherein, perchance,
Will-o'-the-wisp might wickedly dance;
And wielding it keep him from having a chill
At the menacing sound of 'Whip-poor-will!'
And his flesh from creeping beside the bog
At the harsh, bass voice of the viewless frog:—
In short, he felt that the switch would be
Guard, plaything, business and company!

When he got safe home, and joyfully found
He still was himself! and living! and sound!
He planted the twig by his family cot,
To stand as a monument marking the spot
It helped him to reach: and, what was still more,
Because it had grown by his fair one's door.

The twig took root; and as time flew by,
Its boughs spread wide, and its head grew high;
While the priest's good service had long been done,
Which made the youth and the maiden one;
And their young scions arose and played
Around the tree, in its leafy shade.

But many and many a year has fled
Since they were gathered among the dead.
And now their names with the moss o'ergrown,
Are veiled from sight on the church-yard stone,
That leans away, in a lingering fall,
And owns the power that shall level all

The works that the hand of man hath wrought,
Bring him to dust, and his name to nought.
While, near in view, and just beyond
The grassy skirts of the silver pond,
In its 'green old age,' stands the noble tree,
The veteran Elm of Newbury.

CHANGES ON THE DEEP.

A GALLANT ship! and trim and tight,
  Across the deep she speeds away,
While mantled with the golden light
  The sun throws back, at close of day.
And who, that sees that stately ship
Her haughty stem in ocean dip,
Has ever seen a prouder one
Illumined by a setting sun?

The breath of summer sweet and soft,
  Her canvass swells, while, wide and fair,
And floating from her mast aloft,
  Her flag plays off on gentle air.
And as her steady prow divides
The waters to her even sides,
She passes like a bird, between
The peaceful deep and sky serene.

And now grave twilight's tender veil
  The moon, with shafts of silver, rends;
And down on billow, deck and sail
  Her placid lustre gently sends.
The stars, as if the arch of blue
Were pierced to let the glory through,
From their bright world look out and win
The thoughts of man to enter in.

And, many a heart that 's warm and true
  That noble ship bears on with pride;
While 'mid the many forms, are two
  Of passing beauty, side by side.
A fair young mother standing by
Her bosom's lord, has fixed her eye
With his, upon the blessed star
That points them to their home afar.

Their thoughts fly forth to those, who there
  Are waiting now, with joy to hail
The moment that shall grant their prayer,
  And heave in sight their coming sail.
For, many a time the changeful queen
Of night has vanished, and been seen
Since o'er a foreign shore to roam,
They passed from that dear, native home.

The babe, that on its father's breast,
  Has let its little eyelids close,
The mother bears below to rest,
  And sinks with it in sweet repose.
The while a sailor climbs the shroud,
And in the distance spies a cloud:
Low, like a swelling seed it lies
From which the towering storm shall rise.

The powers of air are now about
  To muster from their hidden caves;
The winds unchained come rushing out,
  And into mountains heap the waves.

Upon the sky the darkness spreads!
The tempest on the ocean treads;
And yawning caverns are its track
Amid the waters wild and black.

Its voice — but, who shall give the sounds
  Of that dread voice? — The ship is dashed
In roaring depths — and now, she bounds
  On high, by foaming surges lashed.
And how is she the storm to bide?
Its sweeping wings are strong and wide!
The hand of man has lost control
O'er her! — his work is for the soul!

She 's in a scene of nature's war.
  The winds and waters are at strife;
And both with her, contending for
  The brittle thread of human life
That she contains; while sail and shroud
Have yielded; and her head is bowed.
Then, who that slender thread shall keep,
But He, whose finger moves the deep?

A moment — and the angry blast
  Has done its work and hurried on.
With broken cables, shivered mast;
  With riven sides, and anchor gone,
Behold the ship in ruin lie,
While from the waves a piercing cry
Surmounts the tumult high and wild,
And sounds to heaven, 'My child! my child!'

The mother in the whelming surge
  Lifts up her infant o'er the sea,
While lying on the awful verge
  Where time unveils eternity —
And calls to Mercy from the skies,
To come and rescue, while she dies,
The gift that, with her fleeting breath,
She offers from the gates of death.

It is a call for Heaven to hear.
  Maternal fondness sends above
A voice, that in her Father's ear
  Shall enter quick, for God is love.
In such a moment, hands like these
Their Maker with their offering sees.
And for the faith of such a breast
He will the blow of death arrest!

The moon looks pale from out the cloud,
  While Mercy's angel takes the form
Of him, who, mounted on the shroud,
  Was first to see the coming storm.
The SAILOR has a ready arm
To bring relief and cope with harm.
Though rough his hand, and nerved with steel,
His heart is warm and quick to feel.

And see him, as he braves the frown,
  That sky and sea each other give!
Behold him where he plunges down,
  That child and mother yet may live,

And plucks them from a closing grave!
They 're saved! they 're saved! the maddened
wave
Leaps foaming up to find its prey
Snatched from its mouth and borne away.

They 're saved! they 're saved! but where is he,
Who lulled his fearless babe to sleep?
A floating plank on that wild sea
Has now his vital spark to keep!
But, by the wan, affrighted moon,
Help comes to him ; and he is soon
Upon the deck with living men
To clasp that smiling boy again.

And now can He, who only knows
Each human breast, behold alone
What pure and grateful incense goes
From that sad wreck to his high throne.
The twain whose hearts are truly one
Will early teach their prattling son
Upon his little heart to bear
The SAILOR to his God, in prayer: —

'O, Thou, who in thy hand dost hold
The winds and waves, that wake or sleep,
Thy tender arms of mercy fold
Around the seamen on the deep!

And when their voyage of life is o'er,
May they be welcomed to the shore,
Whose peaceful streets with gold are paved;
And angels sing, "They 're saved! they 're
saved!" '

THE ROBIN'S HYMN.

MY MAKER, I know not the place of thy home;
 If 't is earth or the sky, or the sea.
I only can tell, that wherever I roam
 I 've still a kind father in thee.

I feel that, at night, when I go to my rest,
 Thy wings all around me are flung.
And peaceful I sleep while the down of thy breast
 Is o'er me, as mine, o'er my young.

And when in the morning I open my eye,
 I find thou hast long been awake.
Thy beautiful plumage seems spread o'er the sky,
 And painted again on the lake.

Thy breath has gone into the buds; and the flowers
 Have opened to thee on their stems.
And thou the bright dew-drops hast sent down in showers
 To glitter like thousands of gems.

Thy voice with the notes that can only be thine—
 A music 't is gladness to hear,
Comes through the green boughs of the oak and the pine,
 And falls sweet and soft on my ear.

And many a time hast thou stood between me
  And the arrow, that aimed at my heart.
For, though in a form that my eye could not see,
  I know thou hast parried the dart.

I drink from the drops on the grass and the vine,
  And gratefully gather my food.
I feel thou hast plenty for me and for mine ;—
  That all things declare thou art good.

My Father, thy pinions are ever unfurled,
  With brightness no changes can dim !
My Maker, thy home is all over the world.
  Thou 'lt hear then, thy Robin's low hymn !

THE FLY IN THE GLASS LAMP.

Ah! thou lost, unwary thing,
Flutt'ring with a tortured wing—
Crying, with thy little feet
Scorch'd amid surrounding heat!
Poor, unhappy, suffering fly,
What a painful death to die!

Since, so rashly thou hast strayed
'Twixt the funnel and the shade,
In the fiery prison lost,
Now thy life must pay the cost
Of venturing too near the glare,
Dazzling to allure thee there!

Oh! it fills my heart with pain,
Thus to see thee strive in vain
For escape; for I, alas!
Am too small to lift the glass.
Mother says I must not take
Things my little hands might break.

Here she comes! but 't is too late!
Thou, poor thing, hast met thy fate.
Motion ceases—life has fled—
Dropping on the table, dead,
Now I see thee, thoughtless fly!
'T was a foolish death to die.

'Yes, my child, in careless play,
Thus his life is thrown away.
For a thing that pleased the eye
He rushed onward but to die!
Yet, remember, there was none
Warning him the blaze to shun.

'If thou think'st the untaught flies,
For their errors, so unwise,
Let this insect's fall be hence
From temptation thy defence!
On thy heart a picture stamp
Of *the fly about the lamp!*'

THE BEE AND THE CHILD.

Come here, little Bee,
There are fresh flowers by me;
Come, and just let me see
  How your honey is made!
'I can 't, for I fear
That, for coming too near,
I should pay very dear,
  So I can 't — I 'm afraid!'

O, feel no alarm;
Not a leg, nor an arm,
Nor a wing will I harm.
  You may here sip your fill.
'Pretty maid, then I 'll come
Close beside you and hum,
And you shall have some
  Of the sweets I distil.'

Then my trust shall be free
As yours is in me,
And be sure, little Bee,
  That you do 'nt use your sting!
'Oh! no! no! — since I flew
From the cell where I grew,
None has known me to do
  So ungrateful a thing!'

Then why thus supplied
With a sting, but to hide
And to keep it untried,
  Out of sight, little Bee?
'He, who gave me my sting
And my swift gauzy wing,
Bids me not harm a thing
  That would not injure me!'

THE BED ON THE BEACH.

By what rude waves hast thou been tossed,
To gain this quiet beach?
What wide-spread waters hast thou crossed,
This peaceful shore to reach?

An awful secret dost thou tell
About the yawning deep,
That, while her billows war and swell,
They most profoundly keep.

Thou speakest of one whose weary frame
Has sought repose on thee;
But not of kindred, home, or name,
Sad outcast of the sea!

Thou giv'st no record of his birth,
No token of the clime,
Where he was last a child of earth,
Or when he passed from time.

And who must now, on some far shore,
Await the coming sail
Of him, they will behold no more
Till mortal sight shall fail?

For fearful things dost thou present
Before the spirit's view;
The parting bark! the canvass rent!
The helpless, dying crew!

Of one dread scene the fatal whole,
  In thought, I hear and see.
It chills my blood — it makes my soul
  Grow sick to look at thee.

'The seas must render up their dead!'
  Is all thou dost reply;
While o'er thee, cold and restless bed,
  The tide rolls proud and high!

The guilty deep is taking back
  The witness of her wrath,
To bury it with every track
  That marks its troubled path!

THE HALF-MAST FLAG.

How slow yon bark moves o'er the trembling wave,
While her low flag the sighing breezes sweep!
She comes, a mourner, from the new-made grave
Of him whom she has buried in the deep.

With sorrow heavy-laden, she appears;
Beneath its weight must many a spirit bend!
For hope's last ray she comes to quench in tears
At once, for parent, brother, sister, friend.

Their loved one she has left upon her way!—
Low she has laid him in an ocean tomb,
With wat'ry mountains o'er his youthful clay,
Where human sight shall never pierce the gloom.

To eyes that oft have sought her coming sail,
That they again might rest with joy on him,
Her silent signal tells the fearful tale,
While inward anguish turns their vision dim.

Edwin! can virtue, promise, early worth,
And warm affection, such as thine, depart?
Can one like thee be summoned from the earth,
And yet, the living lay it not to heart?

Oh! there is sadness where thy face was seen,
   And lamentation where thy voice was known,
From those who feel the gate of death between
   Thy bright, immortal spirit, and their own.

And like the wailing surges of the sea,
   That o'er thy sleeping clay, unceasing roll,
Sorrow's dark waves, to those who mourn for thee,
   Rise in their might, to overwhelm the soul.

Yet, woe is but for them. For thee, above
   Is joy unmingled, which the blessed know!
Thy voice is tuned to praise eternal love,
   While sighs and sadness fill thy place below.

Long have the bending angels beckoned thee
   To quit this thorny vale and come on high;
Thy years on earth were few—and thou art free
   From pain, from care and every mortal tie!

Yes—thou hast crossed the cold and swelling tide
   Of Jordan, borne upon thy Saviour's breast.
Thou now art safe where every tear is dried,
   Where pain is ended, and the weary rest.

For He who bids the stormy billows sleep,
   Placed his soft hand beneath thy sinking head;
He, thy best Friend, received, upon the deep,
   His own redeemed, from off thy dying bed.

And, shall we wish thy young and blessed feet
  Back from the holy hills they now have trod?
Or hold our own prepared, that we may meet
  Thy sainted spirit in its home with God?

He is Eternal Wisdom — we are dust;
  And meekly at his footstool may we dwell!
His hand lies heavy on us — yet we trust
  In him alone who 'doeth all things well!'

EDWIN! beloved, departed one, adieu!
  Since He, who lent thee, has recalled his own,
We bow in silence, while, to mortal view,
  Clouds and thick darkness hang around his throne!

THE CROSS.*

'T WAS night. In silence the tranquil scene
Of earth lay under a sky serene.
The moon in her peerless beauty shone.
She traversed the ether fields alone,
With mildness sending her silver beams
To glitter and play in the lakes and streams;
While over the slumbering world she cast
Her mantle of light, as on she passed
Across the numberless stars, that strewed
Her path in the calm, deep solitude.

But there was one, at this peaceful hour,
Awake to worship the holy power,
Whose wisdom the firm foundations laid
Whereon the heavens and earth were made;
Who willed; and what to a world was wrought,
Arose from the depth of eternal thought;
Who spake, while Chaos the mandate heard —
And order appeared at his mighty word;
Who marked the space for the spheres to roll;
Who breathed — and man was a living soul!

* Much of the timber taken from the United States Frigate Constitution, while undergoing her late repairs, has been made into various small articles to be preserved as memorials of her services and achievements.

The lady her evening prayer had said,
Had sung her hymn and a tear had shed,
As the sign of her faith she marked and blessed,
Where lightly it lay on her heaving breast;
While, bowed in spirit, she mourned within
That God's fair image, enslaved by sin,
Had caused the stream from the crimsoned tree,
Where death was conquered, and man made free —
That now he must pass to his native skies
Through the blood of a guiltless sacrifice.

The cross she wore was of oaken wood,
That once in a far-off wild had stood:
'T was carved from the heart of the forest king,
And hung o'er hers by a silken string.
But what it had seen in the royal oak,
And since it bowed to the woodman's stroke,
Until to the sacred emblem formed,
And thus by a christian bosom warmed,
She asked; and this did it seem to say,
As on it, sleeping, a moonbeam lay:

'When called from my mother earth, at first
A fair, young shoot from the acorn burst;
And I was there in the infant tree;
Its vital fluid was feeding me.
And when it arose from the tender germ,
To stand in an oak mature and firm,
Its root struck deep and its head towered high,
While I, still hidden from mortal eye,

Was viewed alone by the radiant One
That kindled the stars and lit the sun.

'Unseen I've listened, and fearless heard
The cry of the savage, of beast and bird.
The heavy tramp of the gloomy bear
Has passed by me to his sunken lair;
The wolf prowled 'round me, the eagle screamed,
And near me the blood of their victims streamed.
I've heard the whiz of the Indian's dart,
The deer's last bound as it touched his heart,
And the crackling faggots that then have blazed,
But reached me not with the flame they raised.

'The wounded chieftain has pressed the sod
Beneath me, trusting an unknown God,
That he to a hunting-ground should go,
In the spirit-world, with his shafts and bow;
While death was hastening to dismiss
His blindly wandering soul from this.
And when that warrior-soul had fled,
And under the clods they laid their dead,
Then nature dissolved his mortal part,
To strengthen the oak in its root and heart.

'The scorching heat and the pinching cold
Have only rendered me strong and bold.
The storms of ages have 'round me beat,
But shook me not from my moveless seat.

The hail has rattled, the torrent poured,
The lightning glared and the thunder roared—
The wind with fury has tried its power
In vain, to ruin my strong high tower;
The sick earth opened, and heaved to free
Her fires, but never neglected me.

'And Nature her sweetest sounds has made
About me to play, in my calm, green shade.
The tender mother who found her young
Where o'er them the living veil was hung,
Would tell the joy of her downy breast
In song, while hovering 'round her nest.
The spirit that made the oak his care
Has touched his harp with a hand of air,
To whispering leaves, that danced to hear
The notes of their guardian angel near.

'But Time, who, born with his wings unfurled,
Where new-made matter became a world,
Has never suffered them since to pause,
Decrees, as first of his tyrant laws,
That all they sweep in his powerful range,
Shall take his signet, and yield to change.
And what no element could destroy,
The tree, which the savage beheld with joy,
And left it flourishing high and fair,
The hand of the white man would not spare.

'He came. The might of his arm he tried.
He smote the oak till it bowed and died.

The stately trunk of its head bereft,
When its limbs were lopped and its sides were cleft,
Was forced away from the sylvan scene,
To strengthen the frame of an ocean queen.
When pierced and probed by the cold, blue steel,
They fastened it over her noble keel,
On every side enclosing it tight
From Heaven's free air and its cheering light.

'When far from my own dear forest-ground,
I lay in irons, and firmly bound
To many an aged oak that died
To form that ship in her power and pride,
They gave her the arms of a mighty host,
And called her after Columbia's boast,
The "CONSTITUTION"—and I, in part,
Was nerve and strength to her dauntless heart.
But sad indeed were the scenes they then
Prepared for me in the ways of men!

'An exile, torn from my place of birth,
They now denied me a home on earth,
And hurried me off on the deep, to be
The restless sport of a rolling sea.
But, not the furious waves I crossed,
By winds and waters driven and tossed,
Nor yet the tempest, in all its wrath,
That came to trouble my perilous path,
Was half so terrible, as the strife
Of man with man, and his waste of life.

'When war strode over the yawning flood,
Displaying his garments drenched in blood,
The withering flash of his fiery eye
He gave as a signal for man to die.
His thundering voice for his victims roared—
And forth from their bosoms the life-streams poured!
A shroud for his banner on high he bore,
With death's dread countenance traced in gore.

'He claimed the ship. With his sword unsheathed,
He reapt on the deep, and round her wreathed
The fairest laurels, that spring and grow
Where drop the arms of a conquered foe!
And, dipped in the red and reeking sluice
Of life's warm current at once let loose,
Her palm he raised in victory high;
And bright was her glory to this world's eye,
Though weeds and weeping its light revealed,
As it shone afar from the victor's shield.

'But Time flew on; and the murdered oak
In many a battle was stricken and broke.
By the mouths of its wounds it craved release
From war and the waves, to the earth and peace.
And what it had sought in its strength, and failed,
It asked in its weakness, and thus prevailed.
From bonds and darkness 't was then set free;
And I was cut from its heart to be,
Through joy and sadness, a holy sign
Of the vow, the faith, and the hopes of thine.

'When war and death shall at length be slain,
For the Prince of peace and life to reign—
When sin, nor sorrow, nor pain, nor night,
Can pass the end of the christian fight—
Where earth's vain glory is all forgot
Before his brightness, who changeth not,
May the Spirit that hovers about thee here,
To note the cause of thy falling tear,
Attest to thy counting all as loss,
To follow the LAMB and bear the CROSS!'

THE WANDERING POLE.

A WANDERER over a stranger land,
With a houseless head and an empty hand,
A brow of care and a heart of grief,
He came to my door and asked relief,
While, few and foreign his accents fell
From a faltering tongue his wants to tell.

The vesture that mantled his wasted form,
Was little to shield it from cold or storm,
As slowly 't was borne by the halting limb
The arm of the Russian had given to him
When, deep in his forehead the scar was sunk,
That showed where the lance at his veins had drunk.

And, traced in his visage, I clearly viewed
The marks of a mind by woe subdued—
A wounded spirit compelled to bear
A weary burden of pain and care;
Though man in his might had striven, and failed
To conquer the soul that his power assailed.

I 'd learnt the story of POLAND's wrongs,
From writer, and speaker, and minstrel songs;
When every breeze that had swelled a sail
Had seemed to waft me the piteous tale,
The mortal groan, or the parting breath
Of those it had left on her fields of death.

I 'd heard of her matrons, who nobly sold
Their fine-wrought vessels of silver and gold;
Of her beautiful maidens, who robbed their hair
Of the costly gems that were glittering there
For brother, or lover, or son, to buy
The arms they had borne to the fight, to die.

Her fearless struggle, her hopeless fall,
Her exiled sons; I had heard of all;
But never had seen her fate before,
As pictured in him, who had reached my door;
His looks, like an orphan's, so sadly said
Of his own dear country, 'My mother is dead!'

And could AMERICA's child behold
A sight like this, with a heart so cold
It would not melt, and a balsam flow
In word and deed, till the stranger's woe
Was softened, if pity and human skill
May reach the spirit's deep-seated ill?

But still did I feel how poor and vain
Was human effort to lull the pain
Of him, whom the sleep of the grave alone
Could make to forget the joys he 'd known
And lost for ever; on time's bleak shore
To find home, kindred, and friends no more.

I knew, if backward his eye was cast,
What fearful visions before it passed.

If onward, how lonely, rude and drear
The path to the end of his journey here,
While Hope had nought to his breast to bring,
And Memory only applied her sting.

I almost prayed, as he turned away,
The FRIEND of the friendless to speed the day,
When he should be laid in his final rest;
To give, in his mansions, among the blest,
A home to the great and suffering soul,
That spoke from the eye of the WANDERING POLE.

POCAHONTAS.

Behold the proud chieftain, whose Indian brow
Is knit with a fearful intent.
His spirit untaught in compassion to bow,
Or a higher on earth than himself to allow,
On the blood of the white man is bent.

That chief is Powhattan! His barbarous throng
With savage decorum have met,
And in the dark council been solemn and long;
They 've danced the rude war-dance; they 've sung the wild song,
And Smith, thy last moment is set!

The monarch has given the awful command,
The prisoner before him is led
To the stone, his death-pillow, amid the strong band
The weapon is up in a fearful, red hand,
And ready to fall on his head!

When lo! there darts forth from that terrible crowd
A female's young, beauteous form,
Like the flash that breaks out, throwing off its black shroud,
And leaps to the earth from the fold of a cloud,
Ere the thunder-peal sounds, in the storm.

But not, like the lightning, to kill or to scath,
Comes the bright Pocahontas! She flies,
Like pity's kind angel, with tears on her path,
To fall as a shield from her father's dread wrath,
On the victim who under it lies!

Her arms o'er the form of the prisoner are thrown;
Round his neck falls her long, jetty hair;
On his head lowly laid she has pillowed her own,
While her voice rends the air with its piteous tone,
As she shrieks — 'Father, father, forbear!

'Spare! spare but his life! 't is thy daughter who cries!
Her head must receive thy first blow!
If now by the hand of Powhattan he dies,
The same shade for ever shall darken our eyes;
My blood o'er the white man shall flow!'

The sachem's proud spirit, which lately so wild
Came forth in the flashes of fire
That lit his stern eye, of its purpose beguiled,
Is melted and tamed by the tears of his child,
Who, weeping, looks up to her sire.

'Rise, child of Powhattan!' he cries, 'it is meet
That mercy should conquer in thee;
My own bird of beauty; thy wing was too fleet!
Thy glance is an arrow — thy voice is too sweet!
Rise up, for the white man is free!'

Now harmless the death-weapon drops to the ground
From the grasp of the chieftain's strong hand.
He lifts up his child, and the victim 's unbound,
While sounds of strange gladness are passing around
Where the plumed, painted savages stand.

The soul of a princess indeed was enshrined
In her, who the forest-ground trod;
And since, by the faith of the Christian refined,
She has given her brow at the font to be signed
'Rebecca, a daughter of God.'

WHY DON'T HE COME?

THE ship has anchored in the bay;
They 've dropped her weary wings; and some
Have manned the boat and come away;
But where is he? Why don 't he come?

Among the crowd with busy feet,
My eye seeks one it cannot find.
While others haste their friends to greet,
Why, why is he so long behind?

Because he bade me dry my cheek,
I dried it, when he went from us;
I smiled with lips that could not speak;
And now, how can he linger thus?

I 've felt a brother's parting kiss
Each moment since he turned from me,
To lose it only in the bliss
Of meeting him — Where can he be?

I 've reared the rose, he bade me rear;
I 've learnt the song, he bade me learn;
And nursed the bird, that he might hear
Us sing to him, at his return.

I 've braided many a lovely flower
  His dear, dear picture to inwreathe;
While doating fancy, hour by hour,
  Has made it smile and seen it breathe.

I wonder if the flight of time
  Has made the likeness now untrue;
And if the sea and foreign clime
  Have touched him with a darker hue.

For I have watched, until the sun
  Has made my longing vision dim;
But cannot catch a glimpse of one
  Among the crowd, that looks like him.

How slow the heavy moments waste,
  While thus he stays! Where can he be?
My heart leaps forth; haste, brother, haste!
  It leaps to meet and welcome thee.

'Thou lovely one! the mournful tale
  That tells why he comes not, will make
Thy heart to bleed; thy cheek turn pale!
  Death finds no tie too strong to break!

'The bird will wait its master long,
  And ask his morning gift in vain.
Ye both must now forget the song
  Of joy, for sorrow's plaintive strain,

'The face, whose shade thy tender hand
  Has wreathed with flowers, is changed! But sea,
Nor sun, nor air of foreign land
  Has wrought the change; for where is he?

'Where! ah! the solemn deep that took
  His form, as with their sad farewell,
His brethren gave the last, last look,
  And lowered him down, that deep must tell!

'But ocean cannot tell the whole—
  The part that death can never chill,
Nor floods dissolve; the living soul
  Is happy, bright and blooming still.

'And nobler songs than ever sound
  From mortal voices greet his ear,
Where sweeter, fairer flowers are found
  Than all he left to wither here.

'This, this is why he does not come,
  Whom thy fond eye has sought so long!
Wait till thy days have filled their sum;
  Then find him in an angel throng!'

THE WINTER KING.

O! what will become of thee, poor little bird?
The muttering storm in the distance is heard;
The rough winds are waking, the clouds growing
black!
They 'll soon scatter snow-flakes all over thy back!
From what sunny clime hast thou wandered away?
And what art thou doing this cold winter day?

'I 'm pecking the gum from the old peach tree.
The storm doesn't trouble me — Pee, dee, dee.'

But, what makes thee seem so unconscious of care?
The brown earth is frozen, the branches are bare!
And how canst thou be so light-hearted and free,
Like Liberty's form with the spirit of glee,
When no place is near for thine evening rest,
No leaf for thy screen, for thy bosom no nest?

'Because the same hand is a shelter for me,
That took off the summer leaves! — Pee, dee, dee.'

But man feels a burden of want and of grief,
While plucking the cluster and binding the sheaf!
We take from the ocean, the earth and the air;
And all their rich gifts do not silence our care.
In summer we faint; in the winter we 're chilled,
With ever a void that is yet to be filled.

'A very small portion sufficient will be,
If sweetened with gratitude! — Pee, dee, dee.'

I thank thee, bright monitor! what thou hast taught
Will oft be the theme of the happiest thought.
We look at the clouds, while the bird has an eye
To Him who reigns over them changeless and high!
And now, little hero, just tell me thy name,
That I may be sure whence my oracle came.

'Because, in all weather I 'm happy and free,
They call me the "WINTER KING" — Pee, dee, dee.'

But soon there 'll be ice weighing down the light bough
Whereon thou art flitting so merrily now!
And though there 's a vesture well-fitted and warm,
Protecting the rest of thy delicate form,
What then wilt thou do with thy little bare feet
To save them from pain 'mid the frost and the sleet?

'I can draw them right up in my feathers, you see!
To warm them, and fly away! — Pee, dee, dee.'

THE RISING EAGLE.

My bird, the struggle 's over!
  Thy wings, at length unfurled,
Will bear thee, noble rover,
  Through yon blue, airy world.

Thy fearless breast has shaken
  Earth's dust and dew away;
Thine eye its aim has taken —
  Its mark the orb of day.

Up, up, the faster leaving
  Thy rocky rest below,
A fresher strength receiving,
  The lighter shalt thou go.

The clouds that hang before thee
  Thou soon shalt over-sweep,
Where all is brightness o'er thee,
  To swim the upper deep.

Through seas of ether sailing,
  Thou lofty, valiant one!
The breath of morn inhaling,
  Thy course is to the sun.

The strife was all in lifting
  Thy breast from earth at first.
The poising, and the shifting
  To balance, was the worst.

And so with us; 't is spreading
Our pinions for the skies,
That keeps us low and dreading
The first attempt to rise.

'T is rousing up and getting
Our balance, that we shun;
With thousand ties besetting,
We shrink from breaking one.

But, when we 've fairly started,
And cleared from all below,
How free and buoyant-hearted,
On eagle wings we go!

And as our bosoms kindle
With pure and holy love,
How all below will dwindle,
And all grow bright above!

The world that we are leaving
Looks little in our sight,
While, clouds and shadows cleaving,
We seek the Source of Light.

Rise! timid soul, and casting
Aside thy doubt and fear,
Mount up where all is lasting;
For all is dying here!

Then, as an eagle training
  Her tender young to fly,
The hand, that's all sustaining,
  Will lift thee to the sky.

While higher, higher soaring
  Thou 'lt feel thy cares are drowned
Where heaven's bright Sun is pouring
  A flood of glory round.

THE DEATH OF THE SAGAMORE.

A SCENE OF THE SEVENTEENTH CENTURY.

The servant of God is on his way
From Boston's beautiful shore;
His boat skims light o'er the silvery bay,
While the sleeping waters awake and play,
At the touch of the playful oar.

The purpose that fills his soul is great
As the soul of a man can know;
Vast as eternity, strong as the gate
The spirit must pass, to a changeless state,
And enter, to bliss or woe!

His boat is fast; and over the sod
Of a neighboring wood he hies,
Through moor and thicket his path is trod,
As he hastens to speak of the living God
In the ear of a man, who dies!

Where Rumney's * forest is high and dark,
The eagle lowers her wing,
O'er him, who once had made her his mark;
For the Sagamore, in his hut of bark,
Is a perishing, powerless king.

* For the character and the death-scene of Wonohaquaham, better known as Sagamore John, son of the Squaw-Sachem; and for an account of the Rev. Mr. Wilson's visit to him, in his last moments, at his wigwam on the ground anciently called *Winnisimit*, and *Rumney Marsh*, but now divided between Chelsea and Saugus, see Thatcher' Indian Biography.

At the door of his wigwam hang the bow,
The antler, and beaver-skin;
While he, who bore them, is faint and low,
Where death has given the fatal blow,
And the monarch expires within.

The eye that glanced, and the eagle fled
Away, through her fields of air;
The hand that drew, and the deer was dead;
The hunter's foot, and the chieftain's head,
And the conqueror's arm, are there!

But each its powerful work has done;
Its triumph at length is past;
The final conflict is now begun,
And weeping the mother hangs over her son,
While the SAGAMORE breathes his last!

The queen of the Massachusetts grieves,
That the life of her child must end!
And that is a noble breast that heaves
With the mortal pang on the bed of leaves,
Of the white man's Indian Friend!

The stately form, which is prostrate there,
On the feet that are cold as snow,
Has often sped in the midnight air
A word to the christian's ear to bear,
Of the plot of his heathen foe!

And oft, when roaming the wild alone,
  That generous heart would melt
At the touch of a ray of light, that shone
From the white man's God, till before his throne
  Almost has the Indian knelt.

Yet the fatal fear, the fear of man,
  That bringeth to man a snare,
Has braced his knee, as it just began
To bend; and the dread of a heathen clan
  Has stifled a christian prayer.

But now, like a flood, to his trembling heart
  Has the fear of a God rushed in;
And keener far than the icy dart,
That rends the flesh and spirit apart,
  Is the thought of his heathen sin.

To the lonely spot where the chief reclines
  While the herald of love draws nigh,
The Indian shrinks, as he marks the signs
Of a soul at peace, and the light that shines
  Alone from a christian's eye.

'Alas!' he cries, in the strange, deep tone
  Of one in the grasp of death,
'No God have I! I have lost my own!
I go to the presence of thine alone,
  To scorch in his fiery breath!

'The Spirit, who makes the skies so bright
 With the prints of his shining feet,
Who rolls the waters, kindles the light,
Imprisons the winds, or gives them their flight —
 I tremble his eye to meet!

'When, oh! if I openly had confessed,
 And followed and loved him here,
I now might fly to his arms for rest,
As the weary bird to her downy nest,
 When the evening shades draw near.

'But, grant me the one great boon I crave
 In a great, and an awful hour!
When I shall have sunk in my forest grave,
O take my Boy to thy home, and save
 That beautiful forest flower!

'The God of thy people, the HOLY ONE —
 And the path that shall reach the skies —
Say! say that to these thou wilt lead my son,
That he may not second the race I 've run,
 Nor die, as his father dies!'

'As his father dies!' with the breath that bore
 That sorrowful sound has fled
The soul of a king — for the strife is o'er
With spirit and flesh; and the SAGAMORE
 Is numbered among the dead!

But has he not, by his high bequest,
  Like the penitent on the tree,
The Saviour of dying man confessed;
And found the promise to him addressed—
  '*To-day thou shalt be with me*'?

SISERA.

FROM DEBORAH'S SONG. JUDGES V.

Why tarries Sisera? His mother stands
At the high window, where her eye commands
The hill and vale afar, while waning day
Shows not her son, in all the winding way.

Forth from the lattice goes her earnest cry,
'Where art thou, Sisera? My son, O why,
While o'er the world this solemn twilight steals,
Why tarry thus thy burning chariot wheels?

'When wilt thou come triumphant from the plain,
With Israel's spoils and captives in thy train;
Thy parent's pride, a shouting kingdom's boast,
Thou valiant leader of a dauntless host?

'How went the battle? None will come and tell
Where the dart entered, or the javelin fell;
What shield was shivered, which the trusty sword
That met its aim, or whose the blood that poured.

'If that I gave thee from my own rich veins
Empurple earth's cold sod, what hope remains?
Thy nation's glory must with thee depart;
And one dread swell will burst thy mothers heart!

'But why thy joyful coming thus delay?
Is it to share the spoil, and take the prey?
Dim grows the distance to my weary eye;
Nor hoof, nor wheel, nor foot of man comes nigh!'

Why, hapless mother, does he not return!
Go to the Kenite's distant place, and learn!
Fly to the tent on Zaanaim's plain;
Ask Heber's wife for him thou call'st in vain!

Enter her tent, and slowly raise the veil;
Lift that spread mantle; see the fatal nail!
Behold thy son, as now he lieth low;
Inglorious chief! and by a woman's blow!

Is this the brow that thou hast hoped to see
Twined with the laurel, high in victory?
The blood thou gav'st him in a form so fair
Is thick around it, on the matted hair!

Pierced through the temples! pillowed on the ground!
Is this the head that glory should have crowned?
Was the fair captive's needle-work to deck,
With many colors, this poor severed neck?

Oh! 't is a fearful thing to be a rod
Used on a people, by the hand of God,
To bring his children back, when they offend;
To chasten them; then have the scourge's end!

To Tabor's mount the bands of Barak drew,
In arms but feeble; in their numbers, few;
While Jabin's hosts, with Sisera their head,
By Kishon's stream the valley overspread.

With strong war-chariots they took the field;
With prancing horses, gleaming spear and shield.
Thick as the grass they overran the plain,
Like that, when mown, to strow it with the slain.

When to the onset, like a stream that gushed
Forth from the mount, the men of Israel rushed;
The Lord of hosts was with them in the fight,
And death, or dread seized every Canaanite.

The ancient river felt its heavy tide
Swell with the blood that flowed upon its side.
Horses and horsemen weltered in the waves,
That bore down thousands into restless graves.

Then Sisera, unchiefed, with none to head,
Leaped from his iron chariot and fled.
His steps the fugitive in terror bent
To ask of Jael refuge in her tent.

She gave him milk; and 'in a lordly dish,'
She brought him food; she granted him his wish
Here to be screened from Barak; but his sleep
She fastened on him! it is long and deep!

Oh, Sisera! it was a fearful thing
To be the minion of an evil king;
Against an injured people to contend,
Who had the God of armies for their friend

THE UNCONSCIOUS ORPHAN.

MOTHER, I have found a tear
In your eye! How came it here?
More are coming; now they chase
One another down your face.
How I feel your bosom heave!
What does make you sob and grieve?
Let me wipe your tears away,
Or I cannot go to play.

Why is father sleeping so?
Put me down, and let me go —
Let me go, where I can stand
Near enough to reach his hand.
Why! it feels as stiff and cold
As a piece of ice, to hold!
Lift me up to kiss his cheek;
Then, perhaps, he 'll wake and speak.

Mother, oh! it is n't he,
For he will not look at me!
Father had n't cheeks so white!
See, the lips are fastened tight!
Father always spoke and smiled,
Calling me his 'darling child;'
He would give and ask a kiss,
When I came; but who is this?

If 't is father, has he done
Speaking to his little one?
Will he never, never more
Know and love me, as before?
Could he hear what we have said?
Tell me; what is being dead?
O! he does 'nt breathe a breath!
Mother, what 's the cause of death?

THE DREAM.

I DREAMED, and 't was a lovely, blessed dream,
  That I again my native hills had found,
The mossy rocks, the valley, and the stream
  That used to hold me captive to its sound.

I was a child again — I roamed anew
  About my early haunts, and saw the whole
That fades, with waking memory, from the view
  Of this mysterious thing we call the soul.

A very child, again beside the brook,
  I made my puny hand a cup to dip
Among the sparkling waters, where I took
  Its hollow full and brought it to my lip.

And oh! that cooling draught I still can taste,
  And feel it in the spirit and the flesh.
'T is like a fount, that in the desert waste
  Leaps out, the weary pilgrim to refresh.

The spice of other days was borne along,
  From shrub and forest, on the balmy breeze;
I heard my warbling wild bird's tender song
  Come sweet and thrilling through the rustling trees.

All was restored, as in the sunny day
  When I believed my little, rural ground
The centre of the world, whose limits lay
  Just where the bright horizon hemmed it round.

And she, who was my sister then, but now,
  What she may be, the pure immortals know,
Who, round the throne of the Eternal bow,
  And bathe in glory veiled from all below.

But she was there, who, with her riper years,
  Once walked, the guardian of my infant feet;
Drew from my hand the thorn, wiped off my tears,
  And brought fresh flowers to deck our grassy seat.

I saw her cheek with life's warm current flushed;
  Clung to the fingers that I used to hold;
Heard the loved voice that is for ever hushed;
  And felt the form that long ago was cold.

All I have been and known, in all the years
  Since I was sporting in that cherished spot,
My hopes, my joys, my wishes and my tears,
  As only dreamings, were alike forgot.

'T was this that made my dream so blest and bright,
  And me the careless thing that I was then.
Yet, Time, I would not now reverse thy flight,
  And risk the running of my race again.

The fairest joys that struck their roots in earth
  I would not rear again, to bloom and fade!
I 've had them once, in their ideal worth;
  Their height I 've measured, and their substance
    weighed.

Nor those, who sleep in peace, would I awake
  To have their hearts with time's delusions filled;
The seal, that God has set, I would not break;
  Nor call the voice to lips that he has stilled.

And yet I love my dream — 't was very sweet
  To be among my native hills again;
Where my light heart was borne by infant feet,
  The careless, blissful creature I was then!

Whene'er I think of it, the warm tears roll,
  Uncalled, and unforbidden, down my cheek;
But not for joy, or sorrow. O my soul,
  Thy nature, power, or purpose, who can speak?

THE FLOWERS IN THE CEMETERY.

PEACE keeps the place where we spring up and bloom.
  Kind, gentle angels hover round, to spread
Our tender leaves, and bow us by the tomb
  To pour our freshest odors o'er the dead.

Soft, silent air supplies our vital breath.
  It wafts no sound of tumult, mirth, or strife,
Where, for the mourners, in the land of Death,
  Beneath his throne we open into life.

Praise to our Maker is the holy part
  Assigned to us ; and, while his power we show,
With soothing skill to reach the stricken heart,
  Awhile to lull the throbbing pulse of woe.

We to the eye, that on our native sod
  Retires unseen to shed the dew of grief,
Attest the presence of a perfect God,
  Whose glory shines on every opening leaf.

Who then our beauty can behold, nor feel
  Something, not sadness, but to joy allied,
Upon the wounded bosom sweetly steal,
  Like balm by spirit-ministers applied ?

Tell us, ye sad ones, if it be not thus ;
  Do ye not own this soothing art is ours,
When ye come out to breathe your sighs to us,
  And count your sorrows to your cherished flowers ?

Here do ye find us steady to our trust,
   As sentinels, who stand to guard the dead.
Each has her charge to watch the sacred dust,
   Of some one sleeping in the dreamless bed.

Well is our high and solemn office done.
   Since we were planted, not a foot has crossed
A spot that we have pointed out as one
   Where rests a friend, that ye have loved and lost.

Night falls around us, like a mourner's veil;
   But, though our beauties in the dimness fade,
Still does the pure, free essence we exhale
   Ascend and penetrate the deepest shade.

If thus the better part of those you weep,
   From death and darkness, rose to life and light;
Then lift your hearts from all that earth could keep
   To that blest world where you may re-unite.

Such is the part that we, the humble Flowers,
   Perform; and such the solace we would give
To man, who, while we bloom our few short hours,
   Has yet a whole eternity to live!

McLELLAN'S TOMB.

SAY, may a stranger's trembling hand presume
To twine its humble wreath upon the tomb
Where young McLELLAN'S sleeping clay was borne,
And not be deemed profane by those who mourn?

May thus, the eye, that ne'er beheld his face,
Seek out and fall upon his resting place,
Where nature hangs her fragrant evergreen
To deck Mount Auburn's calm and holy scene?

Then by his tomb a stranger, yet a friend,
To read his name and age I pensive bend,
And o'er the part that is resigned to earth
Pay my soul's tribute to departed worth!

Shall Science mourn the deed that death has done,
And here lament her lost, beloved son,
When he had gained the knowledge pure and high
To fit him long to live, or soon to die?

Shall truth bewail her champion, when the Lord
Gave his young soldier buckler, helm and sword;
But took him, ere he reached the field of strife,
To bear the palm, and wear the crown of life?

Will Earth lament that he, whose feet have prest
Her many lands, is here so soon at rest;
When through her distant windings called to roam,
He still looked up and sought the spirit's home?

Parental fondness and fraternal love,
Weep they, that he is gone to taste alone
The full fruition of his hopes of bliss,
Which from that world he drew to brighten this?

Yes! they may weep, and friendship drop her tears
For one so ripe in worth, so young in years!
For 'Jesus wept!' and those, who would pursue
The path he trod on earth, must sorrow too.

But, though their eyes with nature's mists are dim,
They soon shall brighten; for they follow Him,
Who to a glorious life the dead shall raise,
And on the lips now silent, perfect praise!

Then fare thee well, thou quiet, sacred spot!
Farther 'the stranger intermeddleth not'
With peace like thine! Hence hope and faith shall rise
Where kindred spirits meet beyond the skies.

THE WINTER ROSE.

O, WHY do I hold thee, my fair, only rose,
My bright little treasure — so dear;
And love thee a thousand times better than those,
In thousands, that lately were here?

Because, like a friend, when the many depart,
As fortune's cold storms gather round,
Till all from without chills the desolate heart,
My sweet winter-flower, thou art found!

Because that for me thou hast budded and blown,
I look with such fondness on thee;
That, while I 've no other, I call thee my own,
And feel thou art living for me.

I know thee. I 've studied thy delicate form,
Till reared from the root to the flower,
That opens to-day, in a season of storm!
To brighten so dreary an hour.

How could I so lavishly scatter my sight
On those, that the gay summer-sun
Had nursed with his beams, when I find such delight
In having and loving but one?

And while thou dost modestly blush at the praise,
That thus I in secret bestow,
It heightens thy beauty, and only can raise
The strain, high and higher to flow.

Although thou must droop, as our dearest ones will,
  I 'll tenderly watch thy decline;
And, in thy sad moments, I 'll cherish thee still,
  Because thou hast cheered me in mine.

Then, hallowed like dust of a friend in the tomb,
  I 'll lay thy pale leaves safe away,
Where memory often shall give them the bloom
  That brightened my dark winter day.

THE CHILD ON THE BEACH.

MARY, a beautiful, artless child,
  Came down on the beach to me,
Where I sat, and a pensive hour beguiled
  By watching the restless sea.

I never had seen her face before,
  And mine was to her unknown ;
But we each rejoiced on that peaceful shore
  The other to meet alone.

Her cheek was the rose's opening bud,
  Her brow of an ivory white ;
Her eyes were bright, as the stars that stud
  The sky of a cloudless night.

To reach my side as she gaily sped,
  With the step of a bounding fawn,
The pebbles scarce moved beneath her tread,
  Ere the little, light foot was gone.

With the love of a holier world than this,
  Her innocent heart seemed warm ;
While the glad, young spirit looked out with bliss
  From its shrine, in her sylph-like form.

Her soul seemed spreading the scene to span,
  That opened before her view,
And longing for power to look the plan
  Of the universe fairly through.

She climbed and stood on the rocky steep,
Like a bird that would mount and fly
Far over the waves, where the broad, blue deep
Rolled up to the bending sky.

She placed her lips to the spiral shell,
And breathed through every fold.
She looked for the depth of its pearly cell
As a miser would look for gold.

Her small white fingers were spread to toss
The foam as it reached the strand.
She ran them along in the purple moss,
And over the sparkling sand.

The green sea-egg by its tenant left,
And formed to an ocean cup,
She held by its sides, of their spears bereft,
To fill, as the waves rolled up.

But the hour went round, and she knew the space
Her mother's soft word assigned ;
While she seemed to look with a saddening face
On all she must leave behind.

She searched 'mid the pebbles, and, finding one
Smooth, clear, and of amber die,
She held it up to the morning sun,
And over her own mild eye.

Then, 'Here,' said she, 'I will give you this,
  That you may remember me!'
And she sealed her gift with a parting kiss,
  And fled from beside the sea.

Mary, thy token is by me yet.
  To me 't is a dearer gem
Than ever was brought from the mine, or set
  In the loftiest diadem.

It carries me back to the far-off deep,
  And places me on the shore,
Where the beauteous child, who bade me keep
  Her pebble, I meet once more.

And all that is lovely, pure and bright
  In a soul that is young, and free
From the stain of guile, and the deadly blight
  Of sorrow, I find in thee.

I wonder if ever thy tender heart
  In memory meets me there,
Where thy soft, quick sigh, as we had to part,
  Was caught by the ocean air.

Blest one! over time's rude shore, on thee
  May an angel guard attend,
And '*a white stone bearing a new name*,' be
  Thy passport when time shall end!

THE PILOT LOST.

MARINERS! mariners, what will ye do?
  The distant, fathomless deep ye 've crossed.
Your rock-bound coast has risen to view;
  And what will ye do? for your Pilot 's lost.

He, who had hastened through surge and foam,
  And reef and shallow so freely passed,
To bring your ship with a welcome home,
  Your faithful Pilot is gone at last!

His trusty boat has her trust betrayed!
  Her master has done with the sail and oar.
And he, low under the waves is laid,
  Who guided his thousands safe to shore.

He took his life in his friendly hand,
  When venturing forth your lives to save.
To bring you again to your native land,
  He hurried himself to a watery grave.

On earth's broad bosom no verdant turf
  Was marked for him in his final rest.
The deep green sea and her curling surf
  Have pillowed his head and wrapped his breast!

The waves o'er which he would lightly skim,
  When many a peril for you was run,
Are sounding a requiem over him,
  And wailing the sorrowful deed they 've done.

With the heart of a brother, an eagle's eye,
  And a pilot's hand, when the heavens are dark,
And blast and billow are strong and high,
  Who will now come to your wildered bark?

O, there is One, who the deep can smooth,
  And hush the winds, who will still be nigh!
Listen! your trembling hearts he'll soothe,
  With 'Mariners, be of good cheer—'t is I.'

Trust him while crossing life's stormy sea.
  In every peril he'll lend you aid.
Your pilot through Jordan's waves he'll be.
  Follow him closely and be not afraid!

THE LEAF.

A LEAF! a leaf! it has been torn
From out a volume full and fair.
'T is to a joyful reader borne
By a mild courier through the air.

The author of the book has writ
His shining name upon the leaf;
And blessed import comes in it,
Although the lines are few and brief.

It says, the flood retires! The heads
Of the lost hills again are seen —
That, on their sides the olive spreads
Her fruitful branches fresh and green! —

That He, who has so late revealed
The awful power that arms his hand,
The fountains of the deep has sealed,
And swept the waters from the land!

Thou man of God! while death has reigned
Without the ark, till every soul
Is hurried hence, thy faith retained,
Thy steady trust has kept thee whole.

When God stretched forth his mighty arm
In terrors clothed to impious men,
It shielded thee and thine from harm.
Go forth! Jehovah smiles again.

Look up! the heavens are clear and bright
  With splendor never seen before.
Behold your Lord his promise write,
  That he will drown the world no more!

For this, the richest, purest dies
  That shine in heaven, he softly blends,
And, like himself, from out the skies,
  His bow for man in glory bends.

The humbled earth, baptized, appears
  Washed by the flood from strife and sin.
Beauty and joy shall follow tears,
  And life and praise where death has been.

The Leaf is one from Nature's book,
  Which, with a tender father's love,
Its holy Author wisely took
  To send thee by the peaceful dove!

A MOTHER'S GRIEF AND JOY.

I COULD not lift my voice to sing,
Nor touch my harp, to sweep a string;
And this world's joy and music seemed
As things whereof I had but dreamed.
For Death's pale angel stood so near
My only child, I could but fear
And watch; or, bow my soul in prayer,
That He who governs Death, would spare
My tender infant's life — would save
My heart from bursting o'er its grave.

Ere yet twelve moons had silvered earth,
Since this bright being had its birth —
Before the soft, endearing word
Of 'MOTHER,' from its lips was heard,
The smiles that lit its beaming face
To marks of pain had given place.
Its cheek was wan, its languid eye
Rose feebly, as, to ask me why
I dropped from mine the tear of grief,
And did not give my babe relief.

The skies seèmed overspread with gloom
Deep as the shades that fill the tomb,
And earth's bright blossoms, past away,
While my sweet flow'ret fading lay.

And, when I prayed — 'Thy will be done!'
Strong nature cried, 'O, be it one,
That shall my sinking babe restore!
And, Father, I will ask no more
Than that this froward will of mine
May here be swallowed up in thine!'

I know not how this double prayer
Of little faith and great despair,
Could e'er have reached the mercy-seat
A gracious answer there to meet!
But this sure word rebuked my fears,
'*To reap in joy, ye sow in tears.*'
Then He, who gave it, heard my cries,
And caused the star of hope to rise
Upon my soul with cheering ray,
A blessed herald of the day.

And, since my heavenly Father smiled
And kindly gave me back my child,
The roses that its cheek resume
Have clothed the earth, to me, with bloom!
Its laughing eye to mine, is bright
Enough to fill the world with light!
There 's music on the balmy air;
There 's joy and glory every where!
I 'll wake my harp — my voice I 'll raise
And give to God my hymn of praise.

THE WRECK AT SEA.

THE struggle is over! The storm-cloud at last
Has emptied itself, and the fury is past!
The ship is a ruin! The mariners wait
Their summons to enter eternity's gate.
The remnant of canvass that flaps in the wind,
Their signal of woe, they may soon leave behind
To give its last flutter above the wild surge,
As all it betokens the deep shall immerge.
They see rising round them a chill, restless grave,
While Death loudly calls them from out the hoarse
wave.

'Come to me! come! ye have no where to flee,
But down in the waters for quiet with me!
My thin, winding arms, ever naked and cold,
Have nothing to warm them but what they infold.
My being unlawful I have to sustain
By feeding on life, that from others I drain!
The sweet buds of childhood, youth's beautiful bloom,
And age's ripe clusters I pluck and consume.
I traverse the world by the light that I steal
Alone from the eyes that in darkness I seal!

'In ocean's black chambers I welcome the forms
That rush to my kingdom, through shipwreck and
storms.

The babe never prattles or climbs on the knee
Of him, who is low in the cold, deep sea.
The eye of his widow grows sunken and dim,
With looking and waking and weeping for him.
The parent's fond heart slowly bleeds for the son,
Till I, for my throne, a new trophy have won!
Come! and the mourners away on the shore
Shall never behold you, or hear of you more!'

Hush! hush! thou pale monarch! a voice from above!
It chides thee — its tones are of mercy and love.
Away! king of terrors! In silence retire.
Though high is thy throne, there is one that is higher!
The sinking have looked from the billows that swell
Around them, to Him, who the surges can quell.
And He, who before has the tempest allayed,
And said to the mariner, 'Be not afraid!'
Is now walking over the waters, to tread
Upon the white spray that is pluming thy head!

A sail! ho! a sail in the moment of need!
On yonder mad breakers she 's riding with speed.
A rescue! it comes in the light little boat,
That 's lowered and manned o'er the perils to float.
While life for the perishing, hope for despair,
And joy and reward for affection are there,
With rocking and tossing, as onward she steers,
And shooting and plunging, the wreck as she nears,
One moment, and then the last wave will be crossed!
Yet all is too late if that unit be lost!

The helper and helpless, while panting to meet,
Have sent forth their voices each other to greet.
And when did those voices go out on the air,
An import so great, such an errand to bear?
Emotions too mighty for sound to convey,
Or, long for the spirit to feel in the clay —
A pulse never known in their bosoms before,
Is each proving now, at the dash of the oar.
And sweet to their hearts will the memory be
Of these clasping hands on the wild, deep sea!

SARAH.

SHE had not breathed this world's inclement air
  Till it had chilled, or touched her with a blight.
She had not lived till sorrow, pain, or care
  Had marked her brow, or dimmed her spirit's light.

Beauty and health hung round her infant form.
  Ten hasty summers had not o'er her flown.
Her guileless heart was happy, pure and warm;
  And she believed all others like her own.

She was a shining creature God had lent
  This world awhile, too holy to be given!
And SARAH knew that she was only sent
  To visit earth, and that her home was heaven.

And, finding much to lure and bind her here,
  She smiled on all around her, while within,
Her little angel bosom felt a fear,
  Lest thoughts might enter with the stain of sin.

The things of time, the flowery fields of earth
  Had much to charm; to win her childish love:
But still she doubted if they all were worth
  The brighter scenes that she should find above.

She therefore made her young and tender heart
  A morning off'ring for her God to keep;
So that, if summoned early to depart,
  Upon his bosom she might fall asleep.

Some spirit-messenger of his had come,
  But none knew how, or when, to Sarah's ear,
And told her she had nearly filled the sum
  Of days allotted for her being here!

She startled not at this. The warning word,
  That told the little listener she must die,
Without surprise, without dismay was heard;
  It filled with purer light her joyful eye.

She only sought to soothe her weeping friends,
  Assuring them, that she was now to go
Where, but to enter, were to make amends
  For more than all that man can leave below.

She fell asleep! The gently fleeting breath
  Left her young spirit on a seraph's wing,
Triumphant o'er the grave! The angel Death,
  To her, had neither terrors or a sting!

She was a blessed creature God had sent
  To show what love and beauty dwell on high,
Upon a kind, a holy errand bent;
  To win our love and lure us to the sky!

THE RAIN-DROP AND THE LILY.

A CLOUD, that had hung like a veil o'er the sun,
Was melted, and came to the earth on the run;
When one of its parts, in a round, sparkling drop,
That coursed down the air, on its way made a stop
To crown a fair Lily, that, lowly and pale,
Was bending to pour out her sweets o'er the vale;
Because, not another of all the bright shower
Could bathe, in descending, so lovely a flower.

The Lily was shocked by the signal of state.
She shook when it came, and was bent with its weight.
''T is brilliant and heavy,' she modestly said,
'And must not be worn by so humble a head.
For me, in my simple and plain robe of white,
To wear a gay coronet courting the sight,
It ill would befit!' so, she bowed herself down,
And on a green leaf meekly cast off her crown.

'And now,' said the Drop, 'as it clearly is seen,
The crown was not needed to make thee a queen,
Permit me awhile at thy feet to repose,
A few secret things of my life to disclose;
And then may I sink in the earth, where thy root
Will take me, and let me return in a shoot,
To hang on thy stem in a beautiful bell,
As pure as the one that I laved when I fell.'

The Lily consented. The Drop then began:—
'My birth was before the creation of man!
When darkness was yet on the face of the deep
I lay in its bosom, an infant asleep.
The Spirit moved over us through the black night;
And when my Creator said, 'Let there be light,'
Its first rays awoke me! I sparkled and played,
In praise of the power by whose word we were made.

'And since—but 't would take many lives such as thine,
To learn half the change that has since followed mine!
I 've run in the stream, I have leapt in the fount;
I 've slept in the lake, and have rolled up the mount
In a light curl of mist. I have strengthened the oak,
When o'er its lone head the red thunderbolt broke!
I 've sailed in the cloud, and distilled in the dew.
As old as the world, I 've a form ever new.

'When earth was submerged, I was under the ark,
Combined with my kindred to bear up the bark.
I 've been at the poles. All the zones I have crossed.
I 've fled from the fire and been caught by the frost.
I 've plunged in the avalanche, heaved in the sea;
And ocean's deep things have been open to me.
The ruins unknown, and the treasures untold
That lie in her caverns, 't was mine to behold!

8

'Through groves of rich coral, while winding my way
Where pearls strewed the bed, and the mariner lay,
I bathed his pale lips and his eye's heavy lid,
When all those bright things from its vision were hid,
And cold, rayless orbs seemed to tell me their sight
By Him was recalled, who said, 'Let there be light.'
From scenes deep and sad, to the skies high and clear,
I rose in a vapor to fall in a tear.

'Approaching the earth, where I paused on thy stem,
Transfixed by a sunbeam, I turned to a gem!
That delicate union of water and light,
Where so many beauties and wonders unite,
Was formed on thy head, and disporting its powers
To mark thee the fairest and sweetest of flowers.
And now, the next form that to sight I assume,
I hope will appear on thy stalk, in its bloom!'

The Drop sunk away where the root drew it in.
And ye, who will go, when the lilies begin
Their buds to unfold to the warm, vernal sun,
And look in the vale, ye may there find the one
That cast off her crown; and the Drop will be seen
To rise gently up o'er the leaves fresh and green,
Transformed to a bell of a pure, snowy white;
And still praising Him, who said, 'Let there be light.'

THE SUMMONED.*

A SCENE IN SPAIN.

VALENCIA's streets are thronged. With fearful state
The crowd move on, and pass without the gate.
That ancient city leaving far behind,
Up the rude height the rugged way they wind.
Where yon bold rock its awful forehead rears,
Lashed by the tempests of six thousand years,
And to the yawning depth below looks down
Steadfast and stern, with one eternal frown.

The space between the cliff and that abyss
Is all, between another world and this,
To him who measures it. If human breath
Reach to its end, 't is but a gift to death.
And then the vultures, ravening wolves of air!
Hover around in quest of plunder there,
Where the coy sun has left the cavern, laid
By the dark crag in everlasting shade.

* Ferdinand, while on his march against the Moors, died of an illness which could not be accounted for, on the 17th of September, 1312. His death took place on the thirtieth day from that on which he had caused two brothers to be put to the cruel death, and for the reasons described in this poem; and he was summoned by them a moment before they were hurled from the rock, to meet them before the King of kings, in *thirty days* from that, to atone for the deed. He has since borne in Spanish history the name of *el Emplazado*, the Summoned.

Now to that frowning height the people go
With groanings loud, and imprecations low.
As in that multitude, who took their way
Up the dread mount, where ONE was heard to say,
'Father forgive them!' in this jarring crowd,
Some wag their heads, while some with grief are
bowed;
And mingled sounds of horror, woe, despair,
Triumph and pain oppress the morning air.

The king is there, the jealous Ferdinand,
Fourth of Castile; and there with ready hand
His executioner, for work so fell
'T will wake a laugh where rebel angels dwell.
The hardened earth will blush to give it place.
In blackest lines a hand on high will trace
A record of the deed, which Mercy's tear
May not efface, she cries so vainly here.

'But, who are they—the young, majestic twain
With forms so fair, and loaded with the chain?
All eyes are fastened on them, while their own
Seem, as they move unheeded and alone;
And time's short, narrow vista looking through
At things beyond it, kindled with the view
Till life immortal lent a steady ray
To their white, marble faces!—who are they?'

Two noble brothers, high in rank and power!
Of youth and chivalry the pride and flower.
The Carvajales, loved by all Castile
So much that Ferdinand begins to feel

Upon his haughty head a loosened crown,
And that his throne may shake and cast him down.
Of these two gallant knights he fain would rid
His kingdom, while his jealous fears are hid.

There has been murder near the palace walls!
He, who at evening walked the stately halls
In manly beauty to the festal board,
Where sparkling draughts in golden cups were poured;
Young Benavides, favorite friend and guest,
Whom Ferdinand loved most and served the best,
Retiring from the banquet lone and late,
Has met a fatal dagger at the gate.

There did the menials find him in his gore,
With only time to gasp, and be no more!
But whose bold hand had urged the fatal blade
That on his heart the mortal touch had made,
He gave no sign, no broken accent fell
From off his quivering, ashy lips, to tell.
The name is wrapped in silence, like the clay
That was to death's dark mansion borne away.

At this the stony bosom of the king
Of feeling showed no brightly welling spring,
Whence sorrow's gentle waters forth might pour,
Because his friend, his favorite was no more.
His heart had settled in a sea of pride,
Till every part was cold and petrified.
He felt the blow; but felt it in his brain,
Where flame and frenzy testified the pain.

In wrath he swore, whoe'er had done the deed,
Should take no trial — have no time to plead!
And using this, the murder of his friend,
As means to serve his own ambitious end —
To sate his envy and allay his fears,
He stamped the names of these young chevaliers,
So high and spotless, with the blighting crime
Of launching Benavides out of time.

He knew Alonzo, eldest of the two,
For Benavides's sister bore a true
And ardent love; — that, on the maiden's part,
Fair Violante gave him back her heart.
He knew her brother had opposed the tie,
And marked the lovers with a watchful eye;
That cutting words and slander's arrows came
From him, upon Alonzo's ear and fame.

He called the death, 'revenge for baffled love,
And just contempt;' and using this to prove
The brothers guilty, brought them to his throne,
Where, by his single word and will alone,
He charged them with a blood-stained, murderous hand,
Convicted both; and sentenced them to stand
On that dread cliff, and thence, together hurled,
To take their passage to another world!

The people murmur at their cruel fate;
But still the king is stern and obdurate.

He fears a rescue; and an armed band
Surrounds the prisoners; while with Ferdinand
There moves of guards a long, imposing train
To show death certain, and resistance vain.
In this array the fearful point is gained,
And foremost there, the brothers stand unchained.

Behold them now, upon the dizzy height,
Looking their long adieu to this world's light—
Breathing their farewell breath of nature's air,
With their last earthly footstep taken there!
From life's sad limit, with a solemn tone
And words commanding, while for scenes unknown,
Their guiltless spirits raise a ready wing,
They thus break silence and address the king.

'In thrice ten days from this, king Ferdinand,
A naked soul, we summon thee to stand
Before the King of kings, the Judge Most High,
To answer for the death that thus we die
Without a trial; to the Eternal throne,
For twofold murder, come and take thine own,
Where guilt and innocence the balance weighs!
Remember! meet us there in THIRTY DAYS!'

A moment now in silent prayer they bend,
And to Almighty love and truth commend
Their injured souls, that stainless in the sight
Of Heaven, are calmly poising for their flight.

Then Don Alonzo, taking from his breast
The silken scarf, has on it closely pressed
His pallid lips, which, to a friend that 's near,
Give his last charge designed for mortal ear.

'To Donna Violante carry this,
Tell her it brings Alonzo's dying kiss.
Tell her the heart that beat beneath its fold
Devoutly loved her, till 't was still and cold —
That this warm bosom never could retain
Love for an angel, with a fiend-like stain —
That, by our final prayer, our latest breath,
We both are guiltless of her brother's death!'

All now is ready — now, the awful throw!
Locked in a close embrace the brothers go,
Whirling down! down! — O Nature! from the view
Turn off, for thou art sick and bleeding, too!
Sun, from the earth let now thy glory fail;
In sable clouds thy mid-day splendor veil!
Untimely darkness, come, and like a pall,
O'er the last frightful picture kindly fall!

The dreadful act is closed, the curtain dropped.
But, can the voice of conscience thus be stopped?
Ah, no! Her iron tongue without control
Sounds deep and ceaseless through the haunted soul
Of Ferdinand, the dismal, harrowing chime
Of 'twofold murder!' 'thirty days of time!'
The monarch has no power that voice to still!
The foe within his breast, no arm to kill!

The hasty moon has nearly run her round;
And still he hears the solemn, threatening sound!
He now lies stretched upon a bed of pain,
Wrung at the vitals, tortured in the brain,
By Death's fierce ministers, while struggling life
Forced to succumb, is sinking from the strife,
When, lo! a herald flying to the court,
Some mighty tidings hastens to report!

Now to the king and those around are read
The dying words of one already dead,
Far from Valencia, in a distant clime;—
A man whose soul allied to hidden crime,
Had deep and deadly stains; and when about
To quit her dwelling, could not wash them out,
And going to her place, would leave a sting
Behind her for the bosom of the king.

'THIS TO KING FERDINAND. Read thou, and know,
Of Benavides I, the secret foe,
Long envied his honor near the throne.
And, for the favor thou to him hast shown,
I hated thee; while vengeance on you both
I vowed, and with a desperado's oath!
His life-stream spouted on this hand that writes!
His death is on the spirit that indites!

'I chose an hour well suited to the deed,
Darkness to veil it—torments to succeed,
Could I but send thy minion's giddy soul
Bathed for my purpose, in the maddening bowl,

And reeling forth in that accursed disguise,
To find the worm that never, never dies!
My steady steel was faithful to its trust;
And what was Benavides here, but dust?

'I fled the kingdom, while thy wrath, I knew,
Would soon make thee a haunted murderer too;
That when thy short-lived earthly reign should end,
Hot chains might re-unite thee to thy friend
Where a long train of monarchs writhe and groan
For power perverted and a bloody throne;
And I, the wretched Pedro, may appear
In royal company, who spurned me here!

'I knew the brothers virtuous, holy, high!
Fit for bright angels of the upper sky!
And all the demon in me could not bear
To cut them off from certain entrance there,
By leaving them a longer space below,
To meet temptation — earth's dark ways to know.
Nor would that demon thus unfinished leave
The snare I had begun for thee to weave!

'Two guiltless victims thou hast slain, and now
I see fulfilled the purpose of my vow.
Hope is no more! To be thy fellow-heir
To all the mighty meaning of *Despair*,
I go before thee, only to await
And hail thine entrance through perdition's gate!
Truth stands — earth fails! and from her crumbling brink,
Thus Pedro greets thee — lo! I sink! I sink ——'

'Hold!' cries the king, with wildly glaring eyes,
'Say not, "the worm that never, *never* dies!"
What day is this?' 'The thirtieth from ——'
'Away! out of my sight, thou who would'st name *that* day!
Fly from my presence! palsied be the tongue
And lips whereon that evil sentence hung!
O, for one breath of air to fan my own!
He said, "*For power perverted — bloody throne!* ——"'

'The thirtieth,' still rings through his dying ear.
The forms of sight grow dim and disappear.
His hand in darkness wanders for a hold
It cannot feel; and growing white and cold,
Falls numb and heavy on his heaving breast.
The spring is snapped! the wheels are all at rest!
O power! the eye whose glance was late command,
Can't close itself! Is this proud Ferdinand?

O'erhung with silken drapery, lies the thing
That yesterday was feared, and called a king.
A mightier one than governed wide Castile
Upon that humbled clay has set his seal!
In bitter memory keeping well the day,
The cited spirit took her lonely way!
Earth knows but this — the SUMMONS was obeyed!
Eternal Wisdom veils the rest in shade.

THE SENTENCED.

THEY say the blessed Spring is here,
With all her buds and flowers;
With singing birds and fountains clear,
Soft winds, and sunny hours.
They say the earth looks new and bright,
That o'er the azure sky
The very clouds are fringed with light,
And gaily floating by.

They tell me nature 's full of life,
And man, of hope and joy:
But ah! not so, my widowed wife,
My more than orphan boy!
For, smiling nature cannot give
Such innocence as theirs
To me; nor can she bid me live
In answer to their prayers..

Beyond my dismal prison-bars,
The coy night air steals by;
And but a few pale, trembling stars
Will greet my guilty eye.
Ere thrice the rising morn shall spread
Her mantle o'er the wave,
I shall be numbered with the dead,
And fill a felon's grave!

To thee, alas! my noble son,
  I leave a withered name —
A life, for what thy sire hath done,
  Of bitter, blighting shame!
And thou, to whom I gave a love
  More pure, and warm, and free,
Than e'er I placed on aught above,
  What do I leave to *thee?*

A bleeding heart, that cannot make
  Its throbbing pulses cease:
That ever swells, but will not break —
  A bosom robbed of peace!
A world all filled with prison gloom,
  By Memory's cruel power:
Thou 'lt smell the dungeon in the bloom
  Of every vernal flower.

A pall will hang beside the way,
  Where'er thy feet may go,
Upon the brightest path to lay
  A shade of death and woe.
I leave thee as a tender vine
  That felt the tempest rush,
And fell, with nought whereon to twine,
  For every foot to crush!

These cutting thoughts, while yet I live,
  Will ceaseless anguish bring,
And, in the last, sad moment, give
  To death a double sting.

From them, O heaven! I turn to thee,
  The sinner's friend to seek —
If thou hast pard'ning grace for me,
  O God! my pardon speak.

Thy spirit in the still, small voice,
  O, send with peace to mine;
And let this trembling soul rejoice
  In being sealed as thine!
Then, through the world's dark wilderness
  Be thou my widow's God —
The Father of my fatherless,
  When I'm beneath the sod!

CAPTAIN KIDD.

THERE 's many a one who oft has heard
  The name of Robert Kidd,
Who cannot tell, perhaps, a word
  Of him, or what he did.

So, though I never saw the man,
  And lived not in his day,
I 'll tell you how his guilt began —
  To what it paved the way.

'T was in New York Kidd had his home,
  And there he left his wife
And children, when he went to roam,
  And lead a seaman's life.

Now Robert had as firm a hand,
  A heart as stern and brave,
As ever met in one on land,
  Or on the briny wave.

'T was in the third king William's time,
  When many a pirate bold
Committed on the seas the crime
  Of shedding blood for gold.

So Captain Kidd was singled out
  As one devoid of fears,
To take a ship and cruise about
  Against the Buccaniers.

The ship was armed with many a gun,
  And manned with many a man,
Across the southern seas to run
  To foil the pirate's plan.

But when she long, from isle to isle,
  Without success, had sailed,
And made no capture all the while,
  Her master's patience failed.

The prizes he so oft had sought,
  He found he sought in vain.
And soon a wicked, bloody thought,
  Came into Robert's brain!

His mind he opened to his men;
  And found his guilty crew
Agreed with him, that they, from then,
  Would all turn pirates too!

He threw his Bible in the deep,
  Defied its Author's will,
And, with his conscience put to sleep,
  Began to rob and kill.

And now the desperado reigned,
  A tyrant on the waves,
While they whose blood his hands had stained,
  Went down to watery graves.

No merchant ship could near him go,
  Which he would not annoy;
For Kidd was passing to and fro,
  And seeking to destroy.

He seized the vessel, plunged the knife
  Within the seamen's breast;
And, by a cruel waste of life,
  His evil gains possessed.

He then would make the nearest isle,
  And go at night by stealth,
To hide within the earth awhile
  His last ill-gotten wealth.

Thus many a shining wedge of gold
  This modern Achan hid;
And many a frightful tale was told
  About the pirate Kidd.

But Justice does not slumber long;
  If slow, she 's ever sure.
There 's none too artful, quick, or strong
  For her to make secure.

To Boston, with a brazen face,
  The pirate boldly went,
Where he was seized; and in disgrace
  And chains to England sent.

The captain and his crew were there,
  A solemn, fearful sight,
Resigning life high up in air,
  E'en at the gibbet's height.

For many a year their bodies hung
  Along the river side,
As beacons, showing old and young
  How they had lived and died.

The wealth they hid was never found,
  Though often sought of men.
'T is where they placed it in the ground,
  Till they should come again!

The earth has seemed by heaven constrained
  The treasures to withhold.
That price of blood has none obtained,
  Or used the pirate's gold!

DAVID AND GOLIATH.

Young David was a ruddy lad
  With silken, sunny locks,
The youngest son that Jesse had:
  He kept his father's flocks.

Goliath was a Philistine,
  A giant huge and high;
He lifted, like a towering pine,
  His head towards the sky.

He was the foe of Israel's race,
  A mighty warrior, too.
And on he strode from place to place,
  And many a man he slew.

So Saul, the king of Israel then,
  Proclaimed it to and fro,
That most he 'd favor of his men
  The one, who 'd kill the foe.

Yet all, who saw this foe draw near,
  Would feel their courage fail;
For not an arrow, sword, or spear,
  Could pierce the giant's mail.

But Jesse's son conceived a way,
  That would deliverance bring;
Whereby he might Goliath slay,
  And thus relieve the king.

Then quick he laid his shepherd's crook
  Upon a grassy bank;
And off he waded in the brook
  From which the lambkins drank.

He culled and fitted to his sling
  Five pebbles, smooth and round;
And one of these he meant should bring
  The giant to the ground.

'I 've killed a lion and a bear,'
  Said he, 'and now I 'll slay
The Philistine, and by the hair
  I 'll bring his head away!'

Then onward to the battle field
  The youthful hero sped;
He knew Goliath by his shield,
  And by his towering head.

But when, with only sling and staff,
  The giant saw him come,
In triumph he began to laugh;
  Yet David struck him dumb.

He fell! 't was David's puny hand
  That caused his overthrow!
Though long the terror of the land,
  A pebble laid him low.

The blood from out his forehead gushed,
He rolled, and writhed, and roared.
The little hero on him rushed
And drew his ponderous sword.

Before its owner's dying eye
He held the gleaming point
Upon his throbbing neck to try;
Then severed cord and joint.

He took the head and carried it
And laid it down by Saul,
And showed him where the pebble hit
That caused the giant's fall.

The boy, who had Goliath slain
With pebbles and a sling,
Was raised, in after years, to reign
As Israel's second king!

'T was not the courage, skill, or might,
Which David had, alone,
That helped him Israel's foe to fight
And conquer, with a stone.

But, when the shepherd stripling went
Goliath thus to kill,
God used him as an instrument,
His purpose to fulfill!

THE LIGHT BALLOON.

SPIRITS that dwell in the world of air!
  Your voices and viewless harps attune,
To bid me hail! as I enter there —
  I 'm coming! I 'm coming! the light balloon!

Ye that have flown to seek me here,
  Spread your gentle and buoyant wings,
To waft me off, till I mount and clear
  From the sight and the sound of earthly things!

Now, the mark of a thousand eyes,
  But soon to fade from the mortal view;
Away! away! to the shining skies,
  I, like a spirit, am speeding, too.

Ye who stand on your rolling ball,
  The shadowy earth, the clouds will soon
Lie between us, and hide you all,
  Like an ocean of waves, from the light balloon!

Yonder sable, vapory mass,
  So big with the bolt that would strike me through,
I shall approach, elude, and pass;
  And glide up, up to the pure, bright blue.

My master's trusty and airy boat,
  Gallantly trimmed, my course I keep;
Without a billow beneath, I float,
  A lonely sail, on the boundless deep.

The sun! the sun is my polar star;
  I traverse a sea that has ne'er been crossed!
The earth is gone! I have left it far
  Behind, as a speck, in the distance lost.

Above the walks, and the tribes of men!
  Beyond the traces of human power!
Out of the reach of the mortal ken!
  'T is a perilous, strange, momentous hour!

Now, my maker, I have thee here!
  Pray to thine own, for the needed boon
Of His breath to waft, and His hand to steer,
  To a peaceful haven, thy light balloon!

THE PHILOSOPHER WITH HIS KITE.

FLYING a kite! at a childish play!
  Is FRANKLIN mad? Have his noble powers
Of mind been crushed? Is this the way
  A wise Philosopher spends his hours?

'I am not mad,' he calmly said,
  And gave the line to his silken kite,
As into the regions of air she sped,
  And pulled for more, in upward flight.

'I 'm going to do what none has done,
  Since man has breathed, or the spheres have whirled;
To show the lightning where to run,
  And to turn its point for the rising world!

'The secret sparks, that the vapors wrap
  In their dusky folds, I 'm going to bring
Across my kite with her iron cap,
  And down to me on a hempen string.

'Ere yonder threatening cloud shall wink,
  I 'll make her carry her head so nigh
To its sable face, she shall reach and drink
  At the fiery stream from its awful eye.

'In truth and soberness now I aim,
  Though none before may have aimed so far,
To lead the electric wildfire tame
  Out of the clouds, to fill my jar!

'I 'll bring a debt on the world, and such
As the richest and greatest ne'er can pay,
Till they for posterity do as much
As, flying my kite, I do to-day!'

THE STEAM-BOAT.

If ever I venture again on the deep,
And hope, with the night, for the blessings of sleep—
To die to the real, and live in a dream,
I'll not clear the land in a boat pushed by steam,
To suffer the torture the helpless one feels,
Entrapped in a ship made to run upon wheels!

Can this be the wave with its light, foamy wreath,
So much like a hard, rocky mountain, beneath
The thundering keel and my quivering berth,
That seem undergoing a quake of the earth,
The while this sea-monster, with bowels of fire,
Is jarring one's head like a toy upon wire?

The creaking and dashing from timber and flood,
And thoughts of the boiler are chilling my blood,
As slowly I measure each wearisome hour,
Deprived of all action, and freedom, and power,
And hope but remains in one glimmering ray,
That breath may be spared till the dawning of day.

While through the long cabin, with pale, dying light,
The dim, lonely lamp, adds but gloom to the night,
At rest on their shelves, its dumb tenants recline
Like those of a tomb, as I view them from mine,
And dare not to slumber, lest nightmare should put
A stop to my heart with her broad, leaden foot.

O come, blessed morning, that I may arise
To breathe the free air, and behold the bright skies!
Return, holy light, and to order restore
The nerves, that were never such rebels before;
And let me go forth with the use of my heels,
To flee from the ship made to run upon wheels.

THE VIOLETS.

Mary, thy violets are bright
 As when, a year ago, I traced
Thy name upon the leaf of white,
 And in its fold thy gift was placed.

Whene'er these cherished flowers I view,
 In form so fair, with living green
And purple, still so rich and true;
 It seems as Mary's self were seen.

I mark again the smile that played
 Upon thy lip, when they were thine;
And hear thy gentle words, that made
 The little fragrant beauties mine.

How sweet it is to have a flower
 Impressed with thoughts of one that 's dear;
To make the past a present hour,
 And hold the absent ever near!

A simple leaf may brush a tear,
 Or chase a cloud of care away—
May touch, with pleasant sounds, the ear,
 Illumine night, and brighten day.

'T will work a charm about the heart,
 And fill with balm its deep regrets.
And such has been the tender part
 Performed by thy sweet Violets!

THE WHITE FLOWER.

She did not know when she gave thee me,
How sweet a comforter thou wouldst be
To her pensive friend in the secret need,
Which the traveller feels from the tramp of steed,
The wavering coach, and a lonely hour
In a stranger group, my fair White Flower!

When the rumbling sound of the wheels was heard,
And made me hasten the parting word,
She plucked thee up from thy native place,
While the soul looked full from her speaking face,
And all she felt at the long farewell,
She left for her tender flower to tell.

Thou beautiful thing! 't was a holy thought,
To give me a work which my Maker wrought;
So pure and perfect to soothe the mind,
In the rattling cage as I sit confined,
While it rolls along in the beaten track,
And my form goes on, but my heart goes back.

I 'll cast my mantle 'twixt thee and harm,
From a neighborly skirt, a hostile arm,
Or a cape astray, whose fall, or brush
Thy delicate head might wound, or crush;
And then, my small, but eloquent friend,
We 'll sweetly commune, to my journey's end.

For He will carry me safely there,
Who made thy slenderest root his care!—
He formed the eye that delights to see,
And the soul that loves to contemplate thee,
We both are the works of his wondrous power;
In silence we 'll praise him, my sweet White Flower.

THE YELLOW BIRD.

They 've caught my little brother,
And he was to me a twin!
They stole him from our mother,
And the cage has shut him in!

I flitted by and found him,
Where he looked so sad and sick,
With the gloomy wires around him,
As he crouched upon a stick.

And, when I tried to cheer him
With the cherry in my bill,
To see me there so near him,
Oh! it made him sadder still.

His tender eye was shining
With the brightness of despair,
With sorrow and repining,
As he bade me have a care!

He said they 'd come and take me,
As they 'd taken him; and then,
A hopeless prisoner make me,
In the fearful hands of men: —

That once in their dominion,
I should have to pine away,
And never stretch a pinion
To my very dying day: —

That the wings that God had made him
  For freedom in the air,
Since man had thus betrayed him,
  Were stiff and useless there.

And, the little darling fellow,
  As he showed his golden vest,
He said beneath the yellow,
  He 'd a sad and aching breast: —

That since he 'd been among them,
  They had ruffled it so much,
The only song he 'd sung them,
  Was a shriek beneath their touch.

How can they love to see him
  So sickly and so sad,
When, if they would but free him,
  He 'd be so well and glad?

My little hapless brother!
  I would fain his bondage share,
I never had another,
  And he 's a captive there!

TO A ROBIN.

Robin, robin, sing to me,
And I 'll gladly suffer thee
Thus to breakfast in the tree,
  On the ruddy cherry.
Soon as thou hast swallowed it,
How I love to see thee flit
To another twig, and sit
  Singing there so merry!

It was kind in thee to fly
Near my window; and to try
There to raise thy notes so high,
  As to break my slumbers.
Robin, half the cheering power
Of this bright and lovely hour,
While I pluck the dewy flower,
  Comes from thy sweet numbers.

And thou wast an honest bird,
Thus to let thy voice be heard,
Asking in the plainest word
  Thou could'st utter, whether
Those, who owned it, would allow
Thee to take upon the bough
Thy repast, and sit, as now,
  Smoothing down thy feathers.

146

Who, that hears the mellow note
From my robin's little throat
On the air of morning float,
  Could desire to still her?
Who her beauty can behold,
And consent to have it told
That he had a heart so cold,
  As to try to kill her?

THE SILK-WORM'S WILL.

On a plain rush hurdle a silk-worm lay,
When a proud young princess came that way ;
The haughty child of a human king
Threw a sidelong glance at the humble thing,
That received with silent gratitude
From the mulberry leaf her simple food,
And shrunk, half scorn and half disgust,
Away from her sister child of the dust;
Declaring she never yet could see
Why a reptile form like this should be;
And that she was not made with nerves so firm,
As calmly to stand by a 'crawling worm!'

With mute forbearance the silk-worm took
The taunting words and the spurning look.
Alike a stranger to self and pride,
She 'd no disquiet from aught beside;
And lived of a meekness and peace possessed,
Which these debar from the human breast.
She only wished, for the harsh abuse,
To find some way to become of use
To the haughty daughter of lordly man;
And thus did she lay a noble plan
To teach her wisdom and make it plain,
That the humble worm was not made in vain;
A plan so generous, deep and high,
That, to carry it out, she must even die!

'No more,' said she, 'will I drink or eat!
I 'll spin and weave me a winding sheet,
To wrap me up from the sun's clear light,
And hide my form from her wounded sight.
In secret then, till my end draws nigh,
I 'll toil for her; and, when I die,
I 'll leave behind, as a farewell boon
To the proud young princess, my whole cocoon,
To be reeled and wove to a shining lace,
And hung in a veil o'er her scornful face!
And when she can calmly draw her breath
Through the very threads that have caused my death;
When she finds, at length, she has nerves so firm,
As to wear the shroud of a crawling worm,
May she bear in mind, that she walks with pride
In the winding sheet where the silk-worm died!'

THE WHIRLWIND.

'Whirlwind, Whirlwind! whither art thou hieing,
Snapping off the flowers young and fair;
Setting all the chaff and the withered leaves to flying;
Tossing up the dust in the air?'

'I,' said the whirlwind, 'cannot stop for talking;
Give me up your cap, my little man,
And the polished stick, that you will not need for walking,
While you run to catch them, if you can!

'Yonder pretty maiden — none has time to tell her
That I 'm coming, ere I shall be there.
I will twirl her zephyr, snatch her light umbrella,
Seize her hat, and brush her glossy hair!'

On went the whirlwind, showing many capers,
One would hardly deem it meet to tell;
Dusting priest and lawyer, flirting gown and papers,
Discomposing matron, beau, and belle.

Whisk! from behind came the long and sweeping feather,
Round the head of old Chanticleer.
Plumed and plumeless bipeds felt the blast together,
In a way they would not like to hear.

Snug in an arbor sat a scholar, musing
 Calmly o'er the philosophic page.
'Flap!' went the leaves of the volume he was using,
 Cutting short the lecture of the sage.

'Hey!' said the book-worm, 'this, I think, is taking
 Rather too much liberty with me.
Yet, I 'll not resent it; for I 'm bent on making
 Use of every thing I hear and see.

'Many, I know, will not their anger stifle,
 When as little cause as this they find
To let it kindle up; but minding every trifle
 Is profitless, as quarrels with the wind!

'Forth to his business, when the whirlwind sallies,
 He is all alive to get it done.
He on his pathway never lags nor dallies,
 But is always up and on the run.

'Though ever whirling, never growing dizzy;
 Motion gives him buoyancy and power.
All who have known him, own that he is busy,
 Doing much in half a fleeting hour.

'O, there is nothing, when our work 's before us,
 Like despatch; for while our time is brief,
Some sweeping blast may suddenly come o'er us,
 Lose our place, and turn another leaf!

151

‘ Whirlwind, Whirlwind, though you ’re but a flurry,
And so odd the business you pursue,
Though you come on, and are off in such a hurry,
I have caught a hint, and now, adieu.’

THE YANKEE TEA-PARTY.

King George sat high on his family throne,
The 'lord of the isles,' that were fairly his own,
And might have sufficed, had his majesty known
The folly of coveting more.
But, seeking a tribute his pomp to maintain,
He reached from his island to grasp at the main,
Intending his coffers should swell with the gain
Brought off from a distant shore.

And when he had summoned in solemn array,
His ministers round him to canvass the way
In which they might make the Americans pay
The costs of the royal court,
'Our liege,' said they, 'there 's many a ship
That might be sent out on an Eastern trip,
And freighted with *tea* for the New World to sip,
And do it for our support.'

''T is done!' said the king, 'and 't is a bright thought!
For this kind of sponging is easily wrought;
The ships shall with Indian leaves be fraught,
And sent to our subject land.
We 'll make Columbia swallow our tea,
And pay the duty, far over the sea,
On every pound, for our "powers that be"
To put in our royal hand!'

And so, in due season, and true royal state,
With their sails puffed out, and their heads held straight,
When the ships rode up, with their well-packed freight,
    To the shores of the western world,
This order imperious echoed around,
'The teas must be bought, and the buyer is bound
To pay us a duty on every pound,'
    As the canvass in port was furled.

But, 'No!' said the Friends in the city of PENN,
'George is a mortal, and Quakers are men!
Your leaves may float off o'er the ocean again;
    For soberly we protest,
That we never will open a traitorous door
To let such a cargo come into a store!
Unentered, unopened, withdraw from our shore
    The treasures of every chest!'

And, 'No!' was the word in the place of the DUTCH;
''T is grinding our faces a little too much,
Broad as they be! and your teas shall not touch
    Our land, while by us it is trod!
The *duty* we owe to ourselves and the throne,
Is, not to be crushed by a foot like our own!
And that of the Briton is quite overgrown.
    We'll have it more tightly shod!'

But the spirited *Yankees* knew just the thing
That would suit themselves, if it did n't the king,
And when the proud sails came flying to bring
    Their freight o'er the glassy bay,

They met and agreed that 't would not be right
His majesty's offer of tea to slight;
For they viewed the affair in a national light,
As they showed in a national way.

They joined in a council; and forming a band
Arrayed like the genuine sons of the land,
In blanket and feather; with hatchet in hand;
And their faces and limbs o'erlaid
With a copper-hued coating of paint, they took
Their way to the ships, while the tomahawks shook;
And their wild '*pow-wow*' made the royalist look
Aghast for the turn of his trade.

'Come,' said the visiters, 'now for our tea!
We 'll take it on deck, if you please, and see,
Of gunpowder, souchong, skin, hyson, bohea,
Which flavor we like the best!'
Then, box after box came up close packed;
And lid after lid was smitten and cracked!
As the red hand worked, and the tomahawk hacked,
And entered the odorous chest.

'This,' said the company, 'this is the way
That we, the YANKEES, are going to pay
Our duty on teas, and help to defray
The cost of the kingly cup.
We 're going to leave every pound to steep,
With its impost on, in the boiling deep —
In a good, strong brine, where we *guess* it will keep
Till the Parliament draws it up!'

Then, over the sides of the ship they poured
The treasures of every box on board,
Till the cargo was out, and the dock was floored
    With the leaves of the Indian tree!
'We'll let,' cried they, 'old England know,
That, bending too much, she may break the bow!
Columbia's spirit can't stoop so low
    As *three pence a pound* on tea!'

THE PIONEERS.

THY waves, proud OHIO, in majesty roll
  Through banks with rich verdure and flowers fitly dressed,
Like the strong tide of mind — like the bright flow of soul,
  That heaves nobly on to the fair, blooming WEST.

Thy music is set to the motion of years,
  Like thee, bearing down to a fathomless flood;
But ours, to the march of the bold PIONEERS,
  Who purchased thy borders with peril and blood.

They fearless went forth where the red heathen foe
  With tomahawk raised, as in ambush he lay,
And poison-tipped arrows to speed from his bow,
  Concealed like a serpent, infested the way.

They saw the tall flame, when the council-fire glared
  Along the deep gloom through the wilderness spread.
They heard the loud whoop, when the knife was prepared
  Its trophy to cleave from the white victim's head!

The apple tree then, 'mid the trees of the wood,
  They reared among savages human and brute,
And felled the dark forest around it that stood,
  To let in the sun-beams, and ripen the fruit.

Their footsteps are traced by the lily and vine;
  Where they lopped the boughs, stands the full-headed sheaf,
And here, from the pillow, the oil and the wine,
  The weary find rest, and the wounded, relief.

Where all was in nature's first wildness and night,
  Till they ventured forth, an invincible band,
The SUN of eternity pours down his light—
  The beauty of holiness spreads o'er the land!

Roll on, proud OHIO! and long as the voice,
  That sounds from thy waters posterity hears,
'T will come in bold numbers to hearts that rejoice,
  In chorus responding, 'The brave PIONEERS!'

REQUIEM FOR LAFAYETTE.

He 's gone to his home! Like a well-ripened sheaf,
The ear in its fulness and sear in its leaf,
The angels have borne him with joy to the skies;
The portals of heaven have closed on their prize.

He 's gone, like the sun at the dying of day,
When shades vale the earth, as his light fades away!
In greatness he rose, and in glory he shone,
Till claimed by the world, while the world was his own.

He 's gone, like the waters in brightness that flow;
While verdure and flowers clothe their banks as they
go,
Till, forth to the deep, in their grandeur they roll;
He 's gone to the ocean, the home of his soul!

He 's gone! and the nations in sackcloth are dressed;
They mingle their tears round the place of his rest:
But none, like Columbia, lingers to weep,
The friend of her youth, with his fathers asleep.

He watched o'er her childhood — he saw her young
form,
Arise in its beauty, 'mid darkness and storm.
Her sighs, like an orphan's, are heavily drawn,
While speaks the cold marble, 'He 's gone! he is
gone!'

LEXINGTON'S DEAD.*

THEY come from the grave to attest to the story
  That we, of their struggle for Liberty, tell! —
From silence and shade, that her mantle of glory
  May fold o'er the first of her Martyrs who fell!

They come, that the balm of her breath may perfume
      them,
  And peacefully then to return to their rest;
That we, from her arms, may receive and entomb them,
  Assured that they once have reposed on her breast.

All hail, sacred Relics! from sixty years' sleeping
  Beneath the green turf, where so freely ye bled;
Who, shrouded in gore, still the battle-ground keeping,
  Forsook not the field, though your vital fire fled!

In valor's proud bed, with its rich purple o'er you,
  The first blood for Freedom that gushed on the sod,
Ye lay, when the souls, to the onset that bore you,
  Had passed with her cause, through your wounds,
      to their God.

* This Ode was sung over the disinterred remains of those who fell in the battle of Lexington, before they were entombed under the monument, on the sixtieth anniversary of the day on which they fell.

Behold, blessed Spirits, who, nobly defending
Your country, rushed forth from your dwellings of clay,
The tribute of sorrow and joy we are blending
To you, o'er their dear hallowed ruins, to pay!

The hearts of a nation, your monument rearing,
Have built it of gratitude, fair and sublime.
It rises to heaven, your honored names bearing,
With earth not to sink, nor to crumble with time.

The ground that, as brothers, in pain ye were sowing,
Imbosomed the seed for a root firm and deep,
When life's crimson fountains were opened and flowing
To moisten the soil for the harvest we reap!

Forgive then the view that we take, ere we sever
From these broken walls, that for us ye forsook!
On them or their like again never, O never,
Are we, or the eye that is mortal, to look!

We give them to earth, till the Saviour, descending
With beauty for ashes, and glory for gloom,
Shall speak, while the dead to his voice are attending,
And life, light and freedom are poured through the tomb!

LIBERTY.

AN ODE FOR THE CELEBRATION OF THE BATTLE OF LEXINGTON.

DEAR is our Liberty,
For great the price that bought her;
And dear the memory
Of those, who nobly sought her!
When war awoke with din and smoke,
By numerous foes surrounded,
With bartered life, they braved the strife,
In death their arms were grounded!
How blest the memory
Of those, who stood defying
The foes of Liberty,
And breathed her name in dying!

Take, holy Liberty,
Their story on thy pinion,
And wing it high and free,
Throughout thy proud dominion!
Their blood was free and warm for thee,
From fearless bosoms streaming,
Like stars, on thine, their deeds must shine,
To all the nations beaming.
Then, keep thy balmy wing
Still growing broad and broader,
And let their story ring
To Earth's remotest border!

Fair daughter of the skies,
As million after million,
In other days, shall rise
Beneath thy wide pavilion,
There may they find their names enshrined,
Their memory, green and spreading,
That all may know to whom they owe
The gifts thy hand is shedding!
O live, sweet Liberty,
The course of time pervading,
Here may thy glory be
Still pure and never fading!

COLUMBIA'S BIRTH-DAY.

AN ODE FOR THE FOURTH OF JULY.

WE hail Columbia's Natal Day,
  And see its glories shine
To light the votive gifts we lay
  At Freedom's holy shrine!
This hallowed day our fathers gave
  The shout of 'LIBERTY!'
And, by their spirits and the glave,
  Avowed their country free!
They fearless then the battle braved,
  And stood the haughty foe.
Where light and high their banner waved,
  They laid oppression low.

But warm the noble hearts that bled
  Where freedom's vot'ries knelt!
Her altar's flame with life was fed
  Their foreign chains to melt.
In blood and death our laurels grew,
  With verdure ne'er to cease:
They shone impearled with sorrow's dew,
  Beside the branch of peace!
On piercing thorns our fathers trod,
  In this bright land of ours,
To soften for their sons the sod
  Now strewed with fruits and flowers.

Then sacred be our Liberty!
  And may its glory beam
On every wave that man shall see,
  Of time's resistless stream!
We bid the children keep in sight
  The spirit of the sire —
To hold the watch-tower, and to light,
  Betimes, the beacon-fire!
We bid the millions, who shall rise
  When we have passed away,
With joy to hail, and ever prize
  Columbia's Natal Day!

WORSHIP BY THE ROSE TREE.

AUTHOR of beauty, Spirit of Power,
Thou, who didst will that the Rose should be,
Here is the place, and this is the hour
To feel thy presence and bow to thee!
Bright is the world with the sun's first rays;
Clear is the dew on the soft, green sod;
The Rose Tree blooms, while the birds sing praise,
And earth gives glory to nature's God.

Under this beautiful work of thine,
The flowery boughs, that are bending o'er
The glistening turf, to thy will divine
I kneel, and its Maker and mine adore.
Thou art around us. Thy robe of light
Touches the gracefully waving tree,
Turning to jewels the tears of night,
And making the buds unfold to thee.

Traced is thy name in delicate lines
On flower and leaf, as they dress the stem.
Thy care is seen, and thy wisdom shines
In even the thorn, that is guarding them.
Now, while the Rose, that has burst her cup,
Opens her heart, and freely throws
To me her odors, I offer up
Thanks to the Being, who made the Rose!

THE MOURNER'S ADDRESS

TO A MINIATURE.

Bright image of her lovely face,
  Who was my spirit's life and light,
'T is agony thy looks to trace, —
  'T is *more*, to have thee out of sight.
To see thee, and remember where
  Thy fair original is laid,
But brings the tortures of despair
  From the sad ruins death has made.

To think how this kind, angel eye,
  Once beamed on me — and then, to feel
How deep the shades that on it lie —
  'T is to my heart like barbed steel.
I have a lock of sunny hair,
  That lay upon this snowy brow;
Its lustre is not dimmed; but where —
  Oh! where 's the forehead's beauty, now?

I have the precious golden band,
  That round her taper finger shone.
The ring is bright; but how 's the hand —
  The hand for which I gave my own?
I have her pledge of early love,
  When Joy's fresh fount was clear and high.
Her gift is near; her soul — above!
  Her form is — where? — earth must reply!

I had a home; and there I found
  Delights like those of Paradise.
Its very name is now a sound
  That chills, when heard, my veins to ice.
My wounded spirit grows estranged
  To all the scenes of life below;
The world and I at once are changed;
  I long a higher home to know.

My love must linger near the dead,
  With fondness that can never die;
Till that which loves and mourns hath fled,
  And dust and dust together lie.
On thee, thou dear, but silent thing!
  I look and doat: Oh! speak to me—
Speak! for my heart, at every string,
  Is wrung, and bleeding over thee!

THE SOLITARY MAN.

He had not sought the joy sublime,
  Nor made the goodly pearl secure,
That will defy the power of time,
  And through eternity endure.
And yet, he needed them ; for all
  His fondly-cherished hopes had fled ;
And peace to him was past recall —
  He lived, while those he loved were dead !

His spirit bowed not in his grief,
  For balm, before his Father's throne.
From sympathy he shunned relief,
  And moved in crowds, but felt alone.
He bent his footsteps to the tomb,
  A sad and solitary man ;
And there, 'mid silence, death and gloom,
  To kindred dust his plaint began.

'I stand, while all around me lie
  Composed in slumber long and deep.
Where darkness sits on every eye,
  'T is mine alone, to wake and weep !
Amid the hearts that once would leap
  In welcome of my coming feet,
I feel my lonely life-stream creep ;
  For not another breast will beat.

'The arms that spread so quick to twine
  Around me, now no more I fill.
The hand, once fondly locked in mine,
  Is here beside me, cold and still.
I sigh, I feel, I think alone;
  For not a dream is passing here.
'T is all oblivion! and my groan
  Unheeded falls on every ear.

'And have the ties affection wove
  So close, so tender, ended thus?
Does nature form our souls for love
  To sport with, and to torture us?
I long this weary load of life
  To lay aside, and be at rest—
To end at once the pain and strife,
  That slowly now consume my breast.

'But earth! earth! earth! it is not so,
  That I may yet thy part dismiss;
And forth to other scenes I go,
  With all my soul confined to this!
For when the busy world shall claim,
  That I amid its throngs appear,
I shall be there in form and name,
  While all beside will linger here.

'I now must join the noisy crowd,
  To hold their pleasures light as air.
Yet, not like one whom grief has bowed,
  Or sorrow marked, will I be there.

The world's rude hand I would not trust
  Too near my bosom's bleeding strings;
For these, beloved and hallowed dust,
  'Twixt God and us are sacred things!

'Its careless eye shall never see
  The wounds it has no balm to heal.
Its look of pity turned on me,
  I would not — could not bear to feel.
Before it I will wear a smile
  To veil the void it cannot fill,
Though deep within my breast the while
  I feel the arrow rankling still.

'The light of mirth may then be found
  Upon my lip, but there alone.
My voice may even mock its sound,
  To drown my weeping spirit's moan.
But, what 's the heartless world to me,
  Since ye, my loved ones, slumber here?
I stand on earth, a blighted tree,
  With winter round me all the year!'

'Thou *barren* tree!' a voice then said,
  And to his soul, 'with leaves and flowers
I 've clothed thee well; and o'er thee shed
  The richest gifts of sun and showers!
And now, if I should cut thee down,
  For giving back no fruit to me,
To lie beneath my withering frown,
  It were not rest and peace for thee!

'An earthly, dark, and sterile heart
  Yields not the fruits of faith and love,
That should, for thine immortal part,
  Be ripened here, and stored above.
Frail man! thy Maker's hand is kind
  In each severe and chastening blow.
The gold that is for heaven refined,
  It tries and polishes below!'

THE CHILD'S ADDRESS TO THE KENTUCKY MUMMY.

And now, Mistress Mummy, since thus you 've been found
By the world, that has long done without you,
In your snug little hiding-place far under ground—
Be pleased to speak out, as we gather around,
And let us hear something about you!

By the style of your dress you are not Madam Eve—
You of course had a father and mother;
No more of your line have we power to conceive,
As you furnish us nothing by which to believe
You had husband, child, sister, or brother.

We know you have lived, though we cannot tell when,
And that too by eating and drinking,
To judge by your teeth, and the lips you *had then;*
And we see you are one of the children of men,
Though long from their looks you 've been shrinking.

Who was it that made you a cavern so deep,
Refused your poor head a last pillow,
And bade you *sit still* when you 'd sunken to sleep,
And they 'd bound you and muffled you up in a heap
Of clothes made of hempen and willow?

Say, whose was the ear that could hear with delight
 The musical trinket found nigh you?
And who had the eye that was pleased with the sight
Of this form (whose queer face might be brown, red,
 or white,)
 Trick'd out in the jewels kept by you?

THE ESCAPE OF THE DOVES.

Come back, pretty doves! Oh! come back from the tree,
You bright, little fugitive things!
We would not have thought you so ready and free
In using your beautiful wings.

We did not suppose, when we lifted the lid
To see if you knew how to fly,
You 'd all flutter off in a moment, and bid
The basket for ever good by!

Come down; and we 'll feast you on insects and seeds;
You sha 'n t have occasion to roam —
We 'll give you all things that a bird ever needs
To make it contented at home.

Then come, pretty doves! O, return for our sakes,
And do 'n t keep away from us thus;
Or, when your old slumbering master awakes,
'T will be a sad moment for us!

'We ca 'n t!' said the birds, 'and the basket may stand
A long time in waiting, for now
You find out too late, that a bird in the hand
Is worth, at least, two on the bough.

'And we, from our height, looking down on you there,
By experience taught to be sage,
Find one pair of wings, that are free in the air,
Are worth two or three in the cage.

'But, when our old master has waked, and shall find
The work you have just been about,
We hope, by the freedom we love, he 'll be kind,
And spare you for letting us out.

'We thank you for all the fine stories you tell,
And all the good things you would give;
But think, since we 're out, we shall do very well
Where nature designed us to live.

'Whenever you think of the swift little wings,
On which from your reach we have flown,
No doubt, you 'll beware, and not meddle with things
In future, that are not your own.

THE TWO THIEVES.

A LADY, they called her Miss Mouse,
In a slate-colored dress, like a Quaker,
Once lived in a snug little house,
Of which she herself was the maker.

There lived in another, close by,
A dame, whom they called Lady Kitty;
But that she was stationed so nigh,
Miss Mouse often thought a great pity.

For she, though so soberly clad,
And never inclined to ill-speaking,
Had often a fancy to gad,
Or, more than her own might be seeking.

She did not then like to be scanned,
Or questioned respecting her duty,
When some little theft she had planned,
Or seen coming home with her booty.

So modest she was, and so shy,
Although an inveterate sinner,
She 'd nip out her part of the pie
Before it was brought up to dinner.

She held that 't was folly to ask
For what her own wits would allow her;
And making her way through the cask,
She helped herself well to the flour.

The candles she scraped to their wicks,
  And full of mischievous invention,
Would do many more naughty tricks
  Which I, as her friend, cannot mention.

Kit too had her living to make,
  And yet, she was so above toiling,
She 'd sooner attack the beef-steak,
  When the cook had prepared it for broiling.

The puss, near a dish of warm toast,
  Has often most patiently lingered,
To seize her first chance; yet, could boast,
  That none ever called her *light-fingered.*

But mending, or minding herself,
  She thought would be quite too much labor,
And so peeped about on the shelf,
  To spy out the faults of her neighbor.

For Mouse loved to peditate there!
  While Kit would watch close to waylay her;
And once, in the midst of her fare,
  Up bounded Miss Kitty to slay her!

But this was as luckless a jump
  As ever Kit made, with the clatter
Of knife, skimmer, spoon, and a thump
  Which she got as she threw down the platter.

While Mouse glided under a dish,
Escaping the mortal disaster,
Miss Kitty turned off to a fish,
The breakfast elect for her master.

Said she to herself, "'t is clear gain,—
This rarity fresh from the water
Will save my white mittens the stain,
And me from the trouble of slaughter!"

But her racket, she found to her cost,
The plot had most fatally thickened;
And all hope of mercy was lost,
As Jack's coming footstep was quickened.

He seized her, and binding her fast,
Declared he could never forgive her;
So Kitty was sentenced, and cast,
With a stone at her neck, in the river!

But Mouse still continued to thieve;
And often, alone in her dwelling,
Would silently laugh in her sleeve,
At the scene in the tale I've been telling.

Till once, by a fatal mishap,
The little unfortunate rover
Perceived herself close in a trap,
And felt that her race was now over.

She knew she must leave all behind;
And thus, in the midst of her terrors,

As every thing rushed to her mind,
  Began her confession of errors.

'You 'll find, on the word of a Mouse,
  Whom hope has for ever forsaken,
The following things in my house,
  Which I have unlawfully taken.

'A cork, that was soaked in the beer,
  Which I nibbled until I was merry;
Some kernels of corn from the ear,
  The skin and the stone of a cherry;

'Some hemp-seed I took from the bird,
  And found most deliciously tasted,
While safe in my covert, I heard
  Its owner complain that 't was wasted;

'You 'll find a few cucumber seeds,
  Which I thought, if they could but be hollowed,
Would answer to string out for beads;
  So the inside of all I have swallowed:

'A few crumbs of biscuit and cheese,
  Which I thought might a long time supply me
With luncheon — some rice and split peas,
  Which seemed well prepared to keep by me;

'A cluster of curls, which I stole
  At night from a young lady's toilet,
And made me a bed of it whole,
  As tearing it open would spoil it;

'And as, in a long, summer day
  I 'd time both for reading and spelling,
I gnawed up the whole of a play,
  And carried it home to my dwelling.

'I wish you 'd set fire to my place,
  And pray you at once to dispatch me;
That none of my enemy's race,
  In the form of Miss Kitty, may catch me!'

Disgrace thus will follow on vice,
  Although for a while it be hidden;
When children, or kittens, or mice,
  Will do what they know is forbidden.

JEMMY STRING.

I KNEW a little heedless boy,
  A child that seldom cared,
If he could get his cake and toy,
  How other matters fared.

He always bore upon his foot
  A signal of the thing,
For which, on him his playmates put
  The name of Jemmy String.

No malice in his heart was there;
  He had no fault beside,
So great as that of wanting care
  To keep his shoe-strings tied.

You 'd often see him on the run,
  To chase the geese about;
While both his shoe-ties were undone,
  With one end slipping out.

He 'd tread on one, then down he 'd go,
  And all around would ring
With bitter cries, and sounds of woe,
  That came from Jemmy String.

And oft, by such a sad mishap,
  Would Jemmy catch a hurt;
The muddy pool would catch his cap,
  His clothes would catch the dirt!

Then home he 'd hasten through the street,
  To tell about his fall:
While on his little sloven feet,
  The cause was plain to all.

For while he shook his aching hand,
  Complaining of the bruise,
The strings were trailing through the sand
  From both his loosened shoes.

One day, his father thought a ride
  Would do his children good;
But Jemmy's shoe-strings were untied,
  And on the stairs he stood.

In hastening down to take his place,
  Upon the carriage seat,
Poor Jemmy lost his joyous face;
  Nor could he keep his feet.

The dragging string had made him trip,
  And, bump! bump! went his head,—
The teeth had struck and cut his lip;
  And tears and blood were shed.

His aching wounds he meekly bore;
But with a swelling heart,
He heard the carriage from the door,
With all but him, depart.

This grievous lesson taught him care,
And gave his mind a spring;
For he resolved no more to bear
The name of Jemmy String!

THE EMIGRANTS FROM THE GRANITE HILLS.

RECITED AT THE BUCKEYE CELEBRATION IN OHIO.

O, WHY do they go, as a lost, roving planet,
A bright group of souls to a region afar,
Like sparks striken out from their own hills of granite,
Combined but to make up a wandering star?

'To find them a home, where the wild deer is leaping
O'er turf that the white man has yet never trod;
Where free and unstartled the foxes are sweeping
The flower from the grass, and the dew from the sod!'

But what will they do, when the heavy rains pouring
Shall stream from the boughs o'er their shelterless heads;
While through the dark forest the night winds are roaring,
And near them the bear, or the Indian treads?

'While echo to echo is merrily telling
The blows, the tall trees in their pride cannot stand,
They 'll smite their firm trunks till they turn to a dwelling
To lodge the bold bosom that 's nerving the hand,'

And what, for a seed-time and harvest to tame it,
  At first will they do with the wild, fallow ground,
While still as the land of his fathers to claim it,
  The savage is gloomily stalking around?

'A price they will offer, and prompt to bestow it,
  To share with the red man the soil for its worth.
But they too are men, and will soon let him know it,
  If still he denies them a portion of earth.'

And what will they do for their sons and their daughters,
  Who hear how their boat glided o'er the blue stream
And touched the wild shore of the soft, curling waters,
  While all seems to them as the things of a dream?

'They 'll leave them a beautiful Eden! and CLIO,
  Delighting to roam o'er a region so fair,
Will waken her lute to the land of OHIO,
  And show the green BUCKEYE LEAF decking her hair!'

THE SPANISH GIRL.

A FAIR, young Andalusian maid
  Was out on the bank of a winding river,
As down through a flow'ry vale it strayed
  To lose itself in the Guadalquiver.
And the girl was chasing a butterfly
Alone, when the son of her king came by.

She ran, while the pure, fresh morning air
  With her light Mantilla's head was playing;
It flushed her cheek; and her raven hair
  In its loosened locks to the wind was straying.
But it never entered the maiden's mind,
That the son of her king was close behind.

But he, while he gazed on her beaming face
  And sylph-like form, felt his heart grow tender.
So he thought, *sub rosa,* he'd watch the chase,
  To see where the hope of her prize would send her.
A clump of flower-shrubs wove a screen,
And he stepped behind it to view the scene.

Though bright were the colors the insect wore,
  The soft black eyes of the maid were brighter;
And light little feet the pursuer bore,
  But the wing of the fugitive still was lighter.
For, every time that it tired and lit,
She crept near enough just to startle it.

At length it tacked with a lazy whirl,
  Like a sportive child with its fellow playing;
While after it ran the delighted girl,
  The whim of a butterfly still obeying.
Intent on the jewel, that charmed her eye,
She still saw not that the prince was nigh.

But soon it lit on an osier bough,
  And seemed, for a moment, calmly sleeping.
Said the joyous girl, 'I will have thee now!'
  But she heeded not that the waves were sweeping
Along the bank, where the osier threw
Its frail arms out, and the tall grass grew.

She gave one bound, and the pleasing snare,
  That the wily insect laid, had caught her;
A quick, faint cry to the passing air,
  And her light young form met the cold, dark water!
But the noble heir of the Spanish throne,
To save her life, quite forgot his own.

For, swift as a dart from the tight-drawn string,
  He flew to the stream for the sinking maiden;
And the youthful arms of the future king
  Came up with their precious trophy laden;
While the wildered girl thought a minister
Of heaven had come down to rescue her.

But soon he proved he belonged to earth,
  And to link her fate to his own besought her.

He gave her the rank of a royal birth,
   As a prince's bride and a monarch's daughter.
The first fair maid ever raised so high
By the playful wings of a butterfly!

THE LOCK OF HAIR.*

NOT the white cov'ring that bespoke
The shroud that wraps her youthful form;
Not the black seal, as slow it broke;
Nor the round tear-drop, quick and warm;

Not these, could that bright lock disguise;
For well I knew it, through them all:
While her glad spirit, from the skies,
Seemed asking, why that tear should fall.

For she, upon whose placid brow
The precious gift so lately shone,
Is crowned with life, an angel now,
In glory near her Maker's throne.

Rejoined to friends, who went before
To lure her to a world of bliss,
She fondly bends, and watches o'er
The loved ones she has left in this.

She points them to the blessed beam
Of that great Sun, whose cheering light
Shone o'er the tide of death's cold stream,
And then dissolved her faith in sight!

* These lines were written on receiving an envelope containing a lock of hair shorn from a beloved friend recently departed.

The well-known lock of auburn hair,
  That once was her's — that now is mine,
Will oft to pensive memory bear
  The lovely, sainted CAROLINE.

THE OLD YEAR'S PRAYER.

With a hoary head,
And with pinions spread
For ever to take its flight,
In pensive mood,
As the Old Year stood
Beside your beds one night —

He said, 'They sleep;
So I will keep
Watch till my hour is o'er;
For, when the hand
Of the clock shall stand
At twelve, I must be no more!

'But I will not break
Their repose, to take
My leave of the race of man;
I will breathe a prayer
On the midnight air;'
And 't was thus his prayer began:

'Author of time and eternity,
Reader of every secret thought —
Thou, who meetest the bound to me,
Giver of all, which the year has brought, —

'May the children that slumber here,
  Sweetly wrapped in their midnight dreams,
Waken to hail a blest New Year,
  With hearts as pure as the morning beams!

'Should they remember an hour, or day
  Of me, which they 've vainly spent, may all
Be forgiven by thee, I pray,
  For the loss of time, which is past recall!

'And by that loss may they learn to prize
  The precious time, that may hence be given;
Regarding every hour that flies
  As a winged minister sent from heaven;

'Some useful lesson, or guiltless joy,
  Or work of virtue, while each may bring,
For the smiling girl and the happy boy
  To snatch for their own from his fleeting wing.

'Now do I hear thy commanding word
  Summon me hence — for my work is done!'
The clock struck twelve! and no more was heard
  Till the voice of the New Year sounded '*one!*'

THE END.

www.ingramcontent.com/pod-product-compliance
Lightning Source LLC
LaVergne TN
LVHW011217110826
845150LV00006B/1452

* 9 7 8 1 4 2 5 5 1 6 6 0 4 *